The Jerusalem Council

THE JERUSALEM COUNCIL

Pastor Ronald D. Kosor

XULON PRESS

Xulon Press
2301 Lucien Way #415
Maitland, FL 32751
407.339.4217
www.xulonpress.com

© 2019 by Pastor Ronald D. Kosor

All rights reserved solely by the author. The author guarantees all contents are original and do not infringe upon the legal rights of any other person or work. No part of this book may be reproduced in any form without the permission of the author. The views expressed in this book are not necessarily those of the publisher.

Unless otherwise indicated, Scripture quotations taken from the New King James Version (NKJV). Copyright © 1982 by Thomas Nelson, Inc. Used by permission. All rights reserved.

Printed in the United States of America.

ISBN-13: 978-1-5456-8189-3

The Jerusalem Council

*The Jerusalem Council was the most important meeting regarding Jews and Gentiles in the history of the world.

*The Jerusalem Council determined how Jews and Gentiles will interpret the Bible forever.

2 Timothy 2:15 (KJV), "study to shew thyself approved unto God, a workman that needeth not to be ashamed, rightly dividing the word of truth."

A special thank you and contact information

Special thanks go to my Father God, my Savior Jesus, and the Holy Spirit who taught me everything I know. I thank my wife Deborah for everything she has done. Rebekah and Gina thank you for all of your efforts. Also a special thanks goes out to all those who have supported our ministries over the years. Please view all of our ministries and you can contact us through any of these. If you would like me to teach, speak, or preach please contact me through these Ministries.

1. You tube search my teaching videos at (Ron Kosor or A Truth Seeker)
2. Outreach Website (www.hisfoodministry.net)
3. Church Website (ALDM.org) (pastor.ron122@gmail.com)
4. International Evangelistic Television Show (crossingpaths.org)

Teamwork makes our dreams work.

I pray this book increases you knowledge and understanding of the Truth of the Word of God. I pray the eyes and understanding of your heart will be opened to receive the Truth.

Maranatha and Shalom!

Table of Contents

A Special Thank / Contact..................................vii
1. Introduction the Jerusalem Council 1
2. The Restoration of All Things................................3
3. Understanding the Difference between Jew and Gentile..........9
4. Pentecost was the beginning of the Messianic Jewish Church ... 13
5. The Jerusalem Council Was and Still Is a Mystery.............. 17
6. The Jerusalem Council Decision and Decrees Regarding Jew
   and Gentile 21
7. The Jerusalem Councils Letter/Epistle....................... 33
8. Galatians Receive the Jerusalem Councils decisions
   (Acts 16:6)... 37
9. Philippians Receive the Jerusalem Councils decisions
   (Acts 16)... 45
10. Thessalonians Receive the Jerusalem Councils decisions
    (Acts 17) 49
11. Corinthians Receive the Jerusalem Councils decisions
    (Acts 18) 53
12. Ephesians Receive the Jerusalem Councils decisions
    (Acts 19) 61
13. The Second Jerusalem Council and Paul's final Journey
    (Acts 20-21) 67
14. The Jerusalem Council Conclusion 73

1.
Introduction the JerusalemCouncil

I have been saved now over 40 years. I have always been an intense studier and student of the Word of God. It was not until I received the revelation and understanding of the Jerusalem Council that I began to understand the Bible entirely. The Bible literally opened up for me. I fully understood and realized how we are to **rightly divide** the Word of God. **2 Timothy 2:15 (KJV), "study to shew thyself approved unto God, a workman that needeth not to be ashamed, rightly dividing the word of truth."** I began to understand the Bible, eschatology, the end times, and the book of revelation. I understood how Jews and Messianic Jews view the same covenants as the Gentiles and born again Christians, but interpret them differently. The Jerusalem council was the council that set in place the most important epistle and letter of the New Covenant.

In this book I will detail for you how The Jerusalem Council changed the world once, and it is getting ready to do it again. Every single Jew, Messianic Jew, Gentile, and Born Again Christian was, and will be affected by it. It was the most important council in the history of mankind. What was the purpose of this meeting? Why was the meeting held? When was the meeting? Who attended the meeting? What specific decisions were made? What is a decree? What was the first New Covenant letter that was written? Who wrote the first epistle? Who was the epistle delivered to? Why was the letter delivered? What impact, if any, did the Jerusalem Council have on the New Covenant? How did this meeting affect Jewish believers? How did the meeting affect Gentile believers? How did this council affect the Messianic Jews? How did the Holy Spirit, apostles, and elders feel about this meeting? This council and its decisions will better help you rightly divide the word of truth regarding these issues and many more. Jews and Gentiles have been dealing with these questions and issues for over 2,000 years. Questions like, eternal security, and once saved always saved just to name a few. **If you do not know the answers to these extremely important questions, this book is for you.** I know the revelation of the Jerusalem Council helped me increase my knowledge and understanding of the bible. I pray it better helps you to understand the position of Jews, Messianic Jews, Gentile and Born again Christians in the Bible. Over forty years of intense bible study is enclosed in this book.

2.
The Restoration of All Things

My first book was Unveiling the New Covenant. Through my studies for my first book I came to the realization of the importance of the Jerusalem Council. Over the past 40 years, I came to the conclusion I would never understand the Bible without understanding the Jerusalem Council, and the impact it had on the early church as well as the church of today. **How will the Jerusalem Council affect Jews, Messianic Jews, Gentiles, and Christians in the last days?** We are in a period of restoration. **Acts 3:21 declares, "Jesus is being held in heaven until the restoration of all things".** To restore something means you must bring it back to its original condition. Here is a very simple example of restoration, God sent Jesus, Jesus sent the Holy Spirit. Now to get back to God we have to go to the Holy Spirit, the Holy Spirit leads us to Jesus; Jesus takes us to the Father God. This process of restoration is exactly what will happen with the Jerusalem Council's decisions and letter that followed. From the death burial and resurrection of the Messiah Jesus Christ till the destruction of the Temple, Jews and Messianic Jews were the majority being saved, and then the Gentiles followed. In the last days of restoration, working backwards the Gentiles will be the majority being saved and the Messianic Jews will follow. **We are seeing this today as the greatest Messianic movement on the earth is happening.** From 70 A.D.–1948 A.D. (1,878 years) there were **no Jews living in Israel,** and Jerusalem was not the capital; therefore, there were not many Messianic Jews living in Israel. Today the world revolves around what happens in Israel. All nations have their eyes focused on Israel. God has miraculously brought Israel back as a nation to fulfill prophecy in these last days. Just take a minute and look at a map. You will see Israel surrounded countries (Turkey, Iran, Iraq, and Egypt) who want to wipe Israel off the map. God has brought them back into their land to fulfill the process of the restoration of all things. Israel had to become a nation again for the Messiah to return to Jerusalem to set up His Kingdom on this earth. This is exactly what we are witnessing today as we see the power and protection of Israel as a nation.

Ezekiel 37:7-11 King James Version (KJV)

⁷ So I prophesied as I was commanded: and as I prophesied, there was a noise, and behold a shaking, and the bones came together, bone to his bone.

⁸ And when I beheld, lo, the sinews and the flesh came up upon them, and the skin covered them above: but there was no breath in them.

⁹ Then said he unto me, Prophesy unto the wind, prophesy, son of man, and say to the wind, Thus saith the Lord GOD; Come from the four winds, O breath, and breathe upon these slain, that they may live.

¹⁰ So I prophesied as he commanded me, and the breath came into them, and they lived, and stood up upon their feet, an exceeding great army.

¹¹ Then he said unto me, Son of man, these bones are the whole house of Israel: behold, they say, our bones are dried, and our hope is lost: we are cut off for our parts.

A few recent Facts regarding the Recent Messianic Movement

* Kehila News Israel, the last professional study was conducted in 1999 by Kai Kjaer-Hansen and Bodil F. Skjott. They found that there were nearly 5,000 believers (both Jewish and non Jewish attending Messianic congregations in the land of Israel.

*In the international Religious freedom report for 2017: Israel Golan Heights, West Bank, and Gaza it says, there is also a community of approximately 20,000 Messianic Jews , as reported by the Messianic Jewish community.

After 1948, actually starting in the late 1960s there has been one of the most powerful movements of God on the earth. **Exactly 70 years after Israel became a nation, Donald Trump, the president of the United States, declared Jerusalem as the capital of Israel. On December 6, 2017 President Trump formally recognized Jerusalem as the capital of Israel and stated that the American embassy would be moved from Tel Aviv to Jerusalem**. The Messianic Jewish Movement is happening right before our eyes. The final stage is being set for the coming of the Messiah, Jesus Christ back to this earth to set up His Millennial Reign of 1,000 years. **For example, CUFI (Christians United for Israel) was established by John Hagee on February 7, 2006, and went from 400 to over 5 million members.** The Messianic Jewish Movement is alive and Gentiles do not know what to do with the Jews who believe in the Messiah. This is exactly what happened in the beginning as the Messianic Jews had to decide what to do with the Gentile who believed in the Messiah. Messianic Jews try to pull Gentiles back to the Torah, Tanakh, and the Old Covenant. Gentiles try to pull the Messianic Jews to the New Covenant and Grace.

* This tug of war has been going on for 2,000 years. I hear **Gentiles** convincingly argue how Israel has been replaced by the Christian Church of today. I hear **Messianic Jews** convincingly argue how the Gentiles are to return to their Jewish roots and observe the Torah and Tanakh. I hear the **Jews** convincingly argue that both of the other parties (Messianic Jews and Gentiles) are following a false God in Jesus Christ. Jews do not believe Jesus was the Son of God.

Please let me give four very important definitions according to the Dictionary and Wikipedia that will better help you understand the importance of the Jerusalem Council. These four groups and their definitions will also better help you understand how to rightly divide the Word of Truth.

*2 Timothy 2:15 (KJV), "study to shew thyself approved unto God, a workman that needeth not to be ashamed, rightly dividing the word of truth."

1. **Jew** (Dictionary); a member of people and cultural community whose traditional religion is Judaism and who trace their origins through the ancient Hebrew people of Israel to Abraham.
2. **Messianic Judaism** (Wikipedia); is a modern syncretic religious movement that **combines Christianity- most importantly, the belief that Jesus is the Messiah-** with the elements of Judaism and Jewish traditions. Its current form emerged in the 1960s and 1970s.
3. **Gentile** (Wikipedia); it is an ethnonym that means non-Jew according to Judaism. **Gentile**, person who is not Jewish. The word stems from the Hebrew term goy, who means a "nation," and was applied both to the Hebrews and to any other nation.
4. **Christian** Chris·tian | \ ˈkris-chən , ˈkrish-\one who professes belief in the teachings of Jesus Christ

My summary is that anyone who is not physically born a Jew, born of a Jewish mother, is a Gentile. A Gentile who accepts Christ as Lord and Savior is a Christian. A Messianic Jew is a Jew who accepts Christ as Lord and Savior. A Jew believes in God, but does not believe in Jesus. A Gentile is any person who is not physically born a Jew. **Every one of these groups could see the same glass half full, or half empty. What I mean by this is they can see the same scriptures but interpret them differently according to what group they**

belong to. The Jerusalem Council and its decisions will reveal the truth regarding this everlasting spiritual tug of war between Jews, Messianic Jews, Gentiles, and Christians. I will show, according to the Word of God, how each party is to <u>rightly divide</u> the Word of God. Did you know that the words circumcised and uncircumcised appear throughout the New Covenant. The New Covenant authors are attempting to get our attention to understand how to rightly divide the Word of Truth for each audience respectively.

The period of the restoration of all things is going to be completed soon and the Jerusalem Council will have much to do with that period of restoration. This book is living proof that it will happen, and it is happening right now. Please understand, I know the most important thing in life for Jews and Gentiles alike is their acceptance of Jesus Christ as their Lord and Savior. I believe after that experience you should be baptized, you should also find a solid Bible-Based Church to learn the Word of God. **Ephesians** 4:13:"till we all come to the unity of the faith and of the knowledge of the Son of God, to a perfect man, to the measure of the stature of the fullness of Christ." Many people have been saved for 40-50 years and have the spiritual maturity of an eight year old. It is my desire that revelations like this will help you grow into a mature man in Christ. **Hebrews 6:1:** " Therefore leaving the elementary teachings about the Christ let us go on to perfection (maturity), not laying the foundation of repentance from dead works and faith towards God, of doctrines of baptisms, laying on of hands, of the resurrection of the dead, and of eternal judgments, and this we will do if God permits." **Also Hebrews 7:22, "by so much more Jesus has become a surety of a better Covenant."** What is the better covenant? **Hebrews 8:6: "… He is the Mediator of a better Covenant, which was established on better promises. For if that first covenant had been faultless, then no place would have been sought for a second." Hebrews 10:9 "…He takes away the First to establish a Second."** The church has been taught so many partial truths. We have taken so many "things" for granted. Just because they have been passed down from generation to generation does not mean they are true. Just because the majority believes in these traditions does not mean they are true either. **Mathew 15:9 (KJV) "in vain they do worship Me, teaching as doctrine the traditions of men".** We need to grow up into a mature man in Christ. What will that look like? What really is the New Covenant? This revelation of the Jerusalem Council will better help you understand. **You will see clearly how the Jerusalem Council changed the course of the World for the early church and it is doing it now for the Church of the last days!**

3.

Understanding the Difference between Jew and Gentile

Jesus knew that the Jerusalem Council had to happen, but He could not tell the disciples this before the divinely appointed time. One of the most interesting scriptures for me in The Bible is **Acts 1:3, "Jesus had to come back for 40 days and teach the disciples "things "concerning the Kingdom of God."** Why would Jesus have to come back for 40 days and teach the disciples "**things**" concerning the Kingdom of God? Remember He talked, taught, and walked with them personally for three and a half years. Logically you would think He would have told them "everything "or taught them everything they needed to know. Obviously, He did not because **He had to come back and teach them** for a period of 40 days in His resurrected body. Could you imagine how powerful that was? What did He teach them? Why 40 days? Throughout the 40 days did Jesus tell the disciples everything that was going to happen in the New Covenant? No, you will see revelation is progressive. The more you accept and learn the more God will give you. **The disciples, Jews, Messianic Jews, and Gentile Christians alike still had to learn "things "as they continue in the New Covenant for the next 25 years until the Jerusalem Council.** From the Feast of First Fruits where Jesus was resurrected on the third day until the Feast of Pentecost you have a total of 50 days. Jesus stayed and taught them for a period of forty days in His resurrected supernatural, immortal body leaving just 10 days to wait in Jerusalem for the Feast of Pentecost. **2 Timothy 2:15 (KJV), "study to shew thyself approved unto God, a workman that needed not to be ashamed, rightly dividing the Word of God."** In order to fully understand the revelation of the mystery of the Jerusalem Council you must understand completely how to rightly divide the Word of God for the Jew, Messianic Jew, Gentile, and Christian. **Messianic Jews, Jews, Gentiles, and Christian believers look at the same bible verses and see different meanings.** One sees the glass half full, the other the glass sees it half empty. They see the scriptures from different angles- same scriptures but different points of view. Please let me give you a simple example. If I say Sabbath, Jews observe from Friday sunset- Saturday sunset. Gentiles say it is Sunday. Messianic Jews could view either way as correct, but mainly will say the Sabbath is from Friday sunset- Saturday sunset. So which view is correct? Let me give you another example using the Feasts of the Lord as an example. First of all, these are not Jewish Feasts; they are the Lord's Feasts. I would like you to see how the Jew, Messianic Jew, Gentile or Gentile Christian view these same scriptures, but they all honor them differently. Each Feast of the Lord has a different meaning depending if you are viewing them- as a Jew, Messianic Jew, Gentile or Gentile Christian. These Feasts of the Lord are found throughout the New Covenant and are also found in **Exodus 23, Leviticus 23:1-44, Numbers 28-29,** and **Deuteronomy 16:1-16.** These are moeds, or divinely appointed days of the Lord. As you will see they are also Holy Convocations, or Holy dress rehearsals that we are to "proclaim" (preach, teach and instruct). Yes, divinely appointed dress rehearsals we are to be preaching, teaching, and instructing people in. Are you? Let's take a quick look at Easter or Passover? When the Messiah Jesus came he **could not** have died on any day. He had to die as the Passover Lamb of God. He had to die on the exact divinely appointed day of the Lord, Abib 14 (the 14th day of the first month). No other day in the entire year would be a fulfillment of the Feast of Passover. Please consider that thought, 360 days in God's Calendar and the Lord had to fulfill the Passover on the Feast of

Passover. There is no way that Jesus, the Lord, was crucified on Friday at three pm placed in Joseph's tomb at 6 pm that evening and resurrected before Sunrise Sunday. Friday evening to Sunday sunrise is not three full days and three full nights.

So what really is the Truth? We have accepted the traditions of men. **Mathew 15:9(KJV) Jesus said, "in vain do they worship me teaching for doctrines the traditions of men".** What other traditions have been passed down that we blindly accept as doctrine? Easter, Ash Wednesday, Good Friday, Seder meals and many other holidays are manmade traditions that have simply been passed down through the years and blindly accepted. We are going to look briefly at the four spring feasts of the Lord to better understand this point of view. How do Jews, Messianic Jews, Gentiles and Christians view the same scriptures and honor them differently?

1. The Feast of Passover is seen by the Jews as their being delivered out of the land of Egypt. Gentiles view this Feast as Jesus' death and resurrection as the Lamb of God. "For God so loved the World that He gave His only begotten Son that whoever believes in Him would not perish, but would have ever lasting life (JOHN 3:16)." Messianic Jews see both sides of the debate as truth. Some see it as Easter?
2. The Feast of Unleavened Bread means the Jews are literally taking leaven out of their houses for seven days. Gentiles view this Feast as Jesus being in the tomb three full days and three full nights. Messianic Jews see both sides of the debate as the truth.
3. The Feast of First Fruits is seen by the Jews as the offering of their first fruits unto the Lord. Gentiles see this as the resurrection of our Lord. Jesus being the first fruits of many brethren. Messianic Jews see both sides of the debate as the truth.
4. The Feast of Pentecost was observed for one thousand five hundred years by the Jews seeing this day as the giving of the law on Mt. Sinai. Gentiles see this as the Day of Pentecost where the

Holy Spirit was sent to the Earth. Messianic Jews see both sides of the debate as the truth .

Jesus had to spend 40 days with His Jewish disciples after His resurrection and teach them things concerning the Kingdom of God because they did not yet fully understand what was going to happen regarding the position of the Jew, Messianic Jew, Gentiles and Gentile Christians in the New Covenant. Each group could read the scriptures and see a totally different meaning. How were the scriptures to be rightly divided and applied to each group was the question 2,000 years ago? That question still arises today. **The Jerusalem Council will answer this 2,000 year old mystery.**

4.

Pentecost was the beginning of the Messianic Jewish Church

Another example of rightly dividing the Word between Jews, Messianic Jews, Gentiles, and Christians lies in the understanding of the first New Covenant church. Did the Gentile Church really begin on the day of Pentecost in Acts chapter 2? **One of the most important aspects of the Feast of Pentecost has been overlooked by the Christian Church.** On the Day of Pentecost, the fulfillment of the Feast of Pentecost, and the first New Testament church headquarters were established in Jerusalem. This church consisted of Messianic Jews. It was not a Gentile church. The first Messianic Jewish church was established on the day of Pentecost, at the feast of Pentecost, and consisted of Jewish believers in the Messiah. **Many think today that Pentecost was the beginning of the Gentile Christian Church.** Pentecost was fulfilled, yes the Holy Spirit fell, but many miss the entire importance of the first Messianic Jewish New Testament Church consisting of Jews who believed in the Messiah. Many take for granted that this first New Testament Church was full of Jews and Gentiles alike, but it was not. **There were only 120 Jews in the upper room.** Only Jews were in Jerusalem celebrating the Feast of Pentecost in Jerusalem. **Remember, we are to know how to rightly divide the Word of Truth. Gentiles would not have been at Jerusalem celebrating the Feast of Pentecost; it was a Jewish Feast (Acts 2)** on the day, the Feast of Pentecost there were Jewish believers in the upper room waiting on the promise just as the Messiah Jesus had instructed them. The fulfillment of the day of Pentecost was not celebrated by Gentiles in Jerusalem. Gentiles did not receive the baptism of the Holy Spirit until **Acts 10, please read** the Great Sheet Revelation and Peter's meeting with Cornelius. **Acts 10:44-46 (NKJV)** "While Peter was speaking these words the Holy Spirit fell upon all those who heard the word and those of the circumcision (Messianic Jews) who had believed were astonished, as many as came with Peter, **because the gift of the Holy Spirit had been poured out on the Gentiles also. For they heard them speak with tongues and magnify God".** Read my first book, *"Unveiling the New Covenant"* for deeper revelation of that mystery. The Jewish believers were astonished because the Gentiles believed and received the Holy Spirit just as the Messianic Jews did on the day of Pentecost 12 years earlier. So for 12 years the Messianic Jews were preaching and only Jews were being saved and filled with the Holy Spirit. You might be asking yourself why he is speaking about these feasts and the day of Pentecost. The main point I am trying to emphasize on here is that we are to rightly divide the Word of truth between Jews, Messianic Jews, Gentiles and Christians. We need to understand how they each view the two covenants of God. **Why would Jesus have to come back for forty days in His resurrected supernatural body and teach the disciples "things" concerning the Kingdom of God?** What other "things" were there that they had to learn as they grew in the faith. Please remember revelation is progressive. The more you receive and accept the more the Lord will show you. In the establishment of the early church you will clearly see that the Jews, Messianic Jews, Gentiles and Gentile Christians had to make very important decisions regarding how each group was to correctly view the Covenants of God. In the early establishment off the New Testament we see four different groups of people viewing two different Covenants of the Lord. Twelve years had passed after Pentecost until the Gentiles believed and received the Holy Spirit with the evidence of speaking in tongues. **Then the Jerusalem Council had their meeting twenty** five years after the Feast of Pentecost to rightly determine how each group was to observe the New Covenant. What were the Jews and Messianic Jews to do with the Gentiles and Gentile Christians?

5.

The Jerusalem Council Was and Still Is a Mystery

Ephesians 3:3, "By referring to this when you read, you can understand my insight into the mystery of Christ". For generations this mystery has been hidden, but now it **has been revealed to the holy apostles** and prophets. To be specific the Gentiles are now "fellow citizens and are of the House of the Lord." What is this mystery? What specifically is the Word referring to here? What was hidden that has now been revealed? " In order to understand the importance of apostleship and how it relates to this revelation let's look at **Galatians 2:7-8** "but on the contrary when they saw that the gospel for the uncircumcised had been entrusted to me (Paul), as the Gospel for the circumcised had been entrusted to Peter. For He who worked effectively in **Peter for the apostleship to the circumcised** (Jews) also worked effectively in **my (Paul) apostleship to the Gentiles.**" So what we see here is that there are two different apostleships. Peter was an apostle to the circumcised, Jewish people. Paul was an apostle to the uncircumcised Gentiles. An apostle is one set apart by God for a specific purpose. These two men were divinely chosen by God to establish the New Covenant. **Always remember Jew and Gentile must first accept Jesus as Lord and Savior. We are discussing the position of the believer Messianic Jew and Gentile Christian alike under the New Covenant.** God chose two different men that represented two different apostleships. They both had their appointed part in the Jerusalem Council, the decisions, and decrees that were decided on. These men were sent specifically to two different groups of people with two totally different commissions. In addition to this, look closely at **Galatians 1:6** "I am amazed that you are turning away so soon from the **Gospel of Christ** to another Gospel, which is really not another; but there are some who trouble you and want to pervert the **Gospel of Christ**". The word **gospel** comes from the Old English god **meaning** "good" and spel **meaning** "news, a story." In Christianity, the term "good news" refers to the story of Jesus Christ's birth, death, and resurrection. **Gospel** music is heard in church and sung by a **gospel** choir. So we can see here that there was a Gospel of Christ, and another Gospel (Old Covenant) that is really not another Gospel. It is the same Gospel, just viewed differently by four different groups of people. The Old Covenant was just a different gospel regarding the Messianic Jews and Gentiles people and how they were to observe it. Let me try to explain this in a simple lay mans words. Peter was an apostle sent specifically to the Jews and Messianic Jews. A Jew will always be a Jew. Those who are physically born a Jew will always be a Jew. They act differently, talk differently, and are different than Gentiles. The Jews or Messianic Jews will always migrate back to their Old Covenant. They will talk about the Torah, the giving of the law (all 613 laws) and the Ten Commandments. Paul was an apostle sent to the Gentiles and Gentile Christians, even though he was born a Jew. **Ephesians 1:1 (KJV) Paul, an apostle of Jesus Christ by the will of God, to the saints which are at Ephesus, and to the faithful in Christ Jesus.** Gentile believers will lean more toward the New Covenant, and the dispensation of grace. Since the writings of the New Covenant this has held true and still holds true today. Consider this thought. The temple was destroyed in A.D. 70 so before this the Jews and Messianic Jews were still entering into the temple and making animal sacrifices. We will examine this more closely later in this revelation of Acts 21. The Gentile believers were never allowed into the temple to offer sacrifices and never will be. There was a special place called the Gentile court for all Gentiles who converted to Judaism to congregate. There was a struggle then and there is a struggle still today between the Jews, Messianic Jews, Gentiles, and Christian believers and how each group is to observe the New Covenant. **Acts 3:21 declares, "Jesus is being held in heaven until the restoration of all things".** To restore something means you must bring it back to its original condition. This is exactly what has been happening in the church since the establishment of the New Covenant. For four thousand years the Jews worshipped and had relationship with Jehovah through the Old Covenant. That is all they knew. When the New Covenant was written, all they had to refer to was the Old Covenant. What were the Jews and Messianic Jews to do with the Gentiles? Could the Jews and Messianic Jews fellowship with Gentiles? Could the Jews eat with Gentiles? If a Gentile transgressed the Sabbath, were they to be killed? Years after the resurrection if a Gentile took the name of the Lord Jehovah in vain were the Jews still to kill the Gentile believer? If a Gentile transgressed the Laws of the Old Covenant after the resurrection and before the destruction of the temple were they to be put to death? Could Gentiles make a blood sacrifice? There was obviously a period here after the Old Covenant and before the finalization of the New Covenant where the Jews, Messianic Jews, Gentiles, apostles and prophets wrestled with these questions. Prophetically, I say this will happen again in the end of the age, at the restoration of all things. Before Jesus the Messiah returns to the earth to set up His Millennial Kingdom the third temple will be built. The Jews will begin to offer the sacrifices of animals according to their Old Covenant again. Some Messianic Jews will also offer blood sacrifices. The church will enter a period just as it was in the beginning regarding these issues. What will the Gentile believers do regarding these animal sacrifices? Will they participate in them? I say absolutely not. For example, we restore a 1957 Chevy; we must bring it back to look like it did in 1957. This is exactly what God has been establishing in the church for the past 500 years through the Protestant Reformation. Let me give a few examples of this concept of restoration. In the beginning God sent Jesus, Jesus then sent us the Holy Spirit. Now if we want to get back to the Father God, we must go to the Holy Spirit first, He takes us to Jesus, Jesus takes us to the Father God. Also consider this truth, in the early church there were mostly Messianic Jews. The Jews had to usher in the Gentiles in the beginning of this dispensation. Therefore, in the end of this dispensation, we, Gentiles, are the majority, and we are witnessing the ushering in of the Messianic Jews conversely. It took **70 years** (until 70 A.D) for the destruction of the temple, and the Messianic Jews were the majority leading Gentiles to repentance in the Gospel of Christ. From 1948 when Israel became a nation) to 2018, another **70 years,** Gentiles have become the majority, and we are now seeing masses of Messianic Jews come into the kingdom of God. Please remember the one example we used, **CUFI (Christians United for Israel) was established by John Hagee on February 7, 2006, and went from 400 to over 5 million members in 2019.** It is the principle of the restoration of all things.

So how did the early church deal with these issues? What did the early Apostolic Messianic Jewish leaders do regarding the Gentile believers in Jesus Christ the Messiah? Just as the Messianic Jews had to deal with the Gentiles in the beginning of the Church age, so will the Gentile Christians have to be able to deal with the Messianic Jews at the end of the age. We see this today in the growth of the Messianic Jewish movement. There is a struggle now for those of the Messianic Jewish movement to pull Gentiles towards the Old Covenant. In the same manner the New Covenant Gentile Christian believers try to pull the Messianic Jews to the New Covenant and the dispensation of grace. The Jerusalem Council will be used to resolve this issue in the final periods of this dispensation. Let us now look at how the Jerusalem Council resolved these issues in the early church.

6.
The Jerusalem Council Decision and Decrees Regarding Jew and Gentile

Twenty-five years after the Day of Pentecost and the beginning of the First Messianic Jewish New Covenant church, two major issues still had to be decided on regarding Gentile believers in the Messiah.

1. Were Gentile believers supposed to circumcise their children?
2. Were Gentiles to observe the Law of Moses?

Webster Dictionary: cir·cum·cise/ˈsərkəm,sīz/

Verb past tense: **circumcised**; past participle: **circumcised**

1. Cut off the foreskin of (a young boy or man, especially a baby) as a religious rite, especially in Judaism and Islam, or as a medical treatment.
2. (As a practice traditional in some cultures) partially or totally remove the external genitalia of (a girl or young woman) for nonmedical reasons.

For me personally, **Acts 15** is the most important chapter in the entire bible. The Jerusalem Council changed the course of the world as well as the church. Please remember, as noted the Jerusalem Council happened twenty-five years after the day of Pentecost and after the establishment of the first New Covenant Church. **For twenty-five years the Messianic Jews who had been taught by Jesus the resurrected Messiah, had no idea what to do with the Gentile believers.** Therefore we can clearly see that there was a distinguishing difference between these four groups of people. The way the Jews and Messianic Jews viewed the New Covenant was different than the Gentiles and Gentile Christians. At first there were only Messianic Jewish Believers and Gentile proselytes. (Gentile Proselytes were basically Gentiles who converted to Judaism). It is extremely important to understand that this is the way it had been for thousands of years. A Gentile had to convert to Judaism. Within this chapter lies the Jerusalem Council, the first epistle of the New Covenant that changed how the world would view the truth of the New Covenant forever. **Acts 15:1, "certain men came down from Judea and taught the brethren; unless you are circumcised according to the customs of Moses you cannot be saved".** There was much debate concerning this issue, so they decided to send Paul, Barnabus, and certain others up to Jerusalem concerning this issue. What issue? Should the Gentile Believers in Jesus Christ the Messiah circumcise their children and do they have to be instructed to follow the laws of Moses in order to be saved? Did they have to convert to Judaism first, in order to be saved? Circumcision was the <u>Old Covenant</u> that God Made with Moses to set His people apart. Why was this an issue? Because according to the Old Covenant the Jews were divinely directed to circumcise their children, and they were taught to observe the laws of Moses. **Genesis 17:10-14, "this is My covenant which you shall keep, between me and you and your descendents after you. Every male child among you must be circumcised…. It will be a sign of the Covenant between Me and you. Every male child among you is to be circumcised on the eighth day".** This is why circumcision was such a requirement for Messianic Jewish Believers in the early church. This was the promise that Jehovah made with the Jewish People, not the Gentiles. Circumcision was an everlasting sign of the covenant or agreement He made with Abraham. The Torah was the only writing the Jews had; it was all they ever had. For four thousand years, anyone who was not circumcised according to these customs was put to death, and cut off from the Jewish people.

Now at the beginning of the New Covenant, Gentiles were being saved and filled with the Holy Spirit. How were the Gentiles to observe the teachings of the Old Covenant? **Please remember this is twenty five long years after the resurrection of the Messiah Jesus Christ.** The Jews and Messianic Jews did not know what to do with Gentiles and Christians. Also, why did they have to go to Jerusalem? As we have noted, the first Messianic Jewish New Covenant Church was established at Jerusalem at the fulfillment of the Feast of Pentecost. Jerusalem is where all the Jewish apostles, disciples, and elders assembled that Jesus had personally taught. This was the headquarters of the first New Covenant Messianic Jewish Church. It was not the beginning of the first Gentile church. Serious questions arose regarding the Gentiles and their position in the New Covenant. What were the Gentiles to do regarding the Old Covenant, circumcision and the laws of Moses? What were the Jews and Messianic Jews to do with all of these new Gentile converts? **If there were no differences between the Jews, Messianic Jews, Gentiles, and Christians there would not be any issues to address.** Everything would just have continued as it had been in the past. The Jews fully understood the Old Covenant and the Gentiles position in that covenant.

Now something different was happening. Remember in Acts 10 where we read about Cornelius, Peter, and the Great Sheet Revelation? For the first time, as a whole, the Gentiles received the Holy Spirit with the evidence of speaking in tongues. This was twelve and a half years after the day of Pentecost, and twelve and a half years before the Jerusalem council. **Look at Acts 10:44-46**, "While Peter was still speaking these words; the Holy Spirit fell on all those who heard the word. And those of the circumcision (Jews) were astonished, as many as came with Peter;

because the Holy Spirit had been poured out on the Gentiles also. For they heard them speak with tongues and magnify God." Gentiles believed, received the Holy Spirit, and were speaking in tongues. What then was to be done with the Gentile believers in the Messiah Jesus Christ? **Acts 15:5, "But some of the sect of the Pharisees who had believed rose up saying it is necessary to circumcise them (Gentiles) and command them (Gentiles) to keep the laws of Moses."** These were Pharisees who had believed in the Messiah, Messianic Jewish believers in the Messiah, and those who knew the Torah and the Old Covenant and the laws of Moses. If this statement was true, there would be no New Covenant. The newly converted Gentiles would have simply converted to Judaism, circumcised their children as was the Jewish custom, and kept the laws of Moses. **That is not what happened.** This is extremely important to remember as we proceed ahead. Paul wrote two thirds of the New Covenant and it all revolves around this one question. **Were the Gentiles supposed to circumcise their children and were they to be taught to observe the Laws of Moses?** Let's take a look at what really did happen. **Acts 15:6,** "now the apostles and elders came together to consider this matter. And when there had been much dispute Peter stood up and said, Men and brethren, you know a good while ago God chose among us that by my mouth the Gentiles should hear the Word of the Lord and believe. So God who knows the heart gave them the Holy Spirit just **as he gave us in the beginning.** He made no distinction between us (Messianic Jews) and them (Gentile Christians) purifying their hearts by faith." We must pause here and look deeper into this part of the Jerusalem Council. **When was the beginning?** Please remember Jesus taught these handpicked, divinely appointed Apostles to go out and evangelize to the world. Jesus taught them for three and a half years in His physical body. Jesus also taught them for forty additional days in His resurrected supernatural body. Acts 1:3 (KJV) "To whom also he showed himself alive after his passion by many infallible proofs, being seen of them forty days, and speaking of the things pertaining to the kingdom of God" They were filled with the Holy Spirit on the Feast of Pentecost. The Jerusalem Council was twenty- five years after the Messiah had taught them "things concerning the Kingdom of God." You would think by now, twenty-five years later that they would know exactly what to do with the Gentile Christians. The beginning here that Peter is referencing is found in **Acts 10:1-45**. Here we see where Peter received the Great Sheet Revelation, when all types of birds, fouls of the air, and creeping crawling things, four footed beasts came down on a great sheet. A voice came from heaven and said, "Peter kill and eat." He said, "by no means Lord for I have never eaten anything unholy common or unclean". Peter recognized the voice as the Lord. This happened three times and the sheet was immediately taken back up into heaven. Peter was then instructed by an angel and sent to Cornelius's house. They had a large meeting at Cornelius' house were Peter came and shared the gospel to Gentiles. As Peter was speaking, the Holy Spirit fell on all those who heard the message, and they began to speak in new tongues. What is interesting and important to realize here is that these were all Gentile believers. This was the first time that a group of Gentiles who were not converted Jews or Proselytes believed in Jesus and received the baptism of the Holy Spirit. Many have been taught the first time this happened was on the day of Pentecost. As we have revealed the day of Pentecost was the fulfillment of the feast of Pentecost, and the Jews were baptized in the Holy Spirit. **Why are these scriptures in Acts 10:1-45 so important?** This meeting with Cornelius happened approximately **twelve and a half years** after the Feast of Pentecost was fulfilled **on the day of Pentecost**. The meeting we are discussing in **Acts 15** regarding Gentiles was approximately twelve and a half years after the meeting with Cornelius. Therefore, there was a **twenty-five year period** between the fulfillment of the Feast of Pentecost in Acts 2, and the Jerusalem council. Please take a moment and consider that thought. Twenty-five years after the Messiah was resurrected from the dead the Messianic Jews still did not know what to do with the new Gentile believers in Christ. I know Jesus could have told the disciples everything regarding the Gentile believers and the New Covenant, but He did not. It was not until twenty-five years later that they were dealing with issues regarding Gentiles. The Jerusalem Council was held to determine this extremely important issue regarding Gentiles and what was to be done with them.

Timeline:
- A.D. 31 *Jesus spends 40 days with disciples teaching them things concerning the Kingdom after His resurrection (Acts 1:3-6).
- 10 days later at the Feast of Pentecost the first New Testament Messianic Jewish church was established in Jerusalem (Acts 2)
- A.D. 43 * Gentile Pentecost/ 12 ½ years later after the Day of Pentecost, Peter has the Great Sheet revelation and preaches at Cornelius house. First time Gentiles are filled with the Holy Spirit and speak in tongues (Acts 10: 1-45)
- A.D. 43-46 Paul and Barnabus preach in Antioch for three years and Disciples are called Christians for the first time (Acts 14:16-28).
- A.D. 55-56 * 12 ½ years after Gentile Pentecost and 25 years after the Messianic Jewish Pentecost the First Jerusalem Council takes place!
- (Acts 15:16-31) Paul separates from Barnabus chooses Timothy
- For 3 years Paul and Timothy journey through the cities delivering the decrees of the Jerusalem Council
- A.D. 58-60 Second Jerusalem Council (Acts 21:18-26). Nothing changes regarding the Decrees the Holy Spirit decided on for Gentiles.

*Approximately 25 years after being taught by the resurrected Messiah and being filled with the Holy Spirit the leading Messianic Jewish apostles and elders did not know what to do with the Gentiles regarding the Old Covenant, circumcision, and commands

to observe the laws of Moses. The Jerusalem Council dealt specifically with these issues. **Acts 15:9** "He made no distinction between us (Messianic Jews) and them (Gentiles) cleansing their (Gentiles) hearts by faith." Wow, here the leading apostles and elders who were at Jerusalem were saying that now, the New Covenant, God was not making any distinctions between Jews and Gentiles cleansing their hearts by faith. The Messianic Jews that observed the Torah, circumcision, and the laws of Moses were now saved and justified by faith just the same way that the Gentiles were. Can you imagine how serious this declaration was? Forevermore Jews would be saved by faith, the same way as the Gentiles. In the previous four thousand years this had **never** been taught through the Old Covenant. **Acts 15:10-11** "Now why therefore do you, place on the neck of the disciples a yoke which neither we nor our fathers were able to bear? But we believe that through the grace of the Lord we (Jews) shall be saved in the same manner as they (Gentiles)." The leading Jewish apostles and elders in Jerusalem are declaring they would now be saved by grace and through faith, not by circumcision and the law. The yoke they, nor their fathers, were able to bear was the keeping of the 613 Laws of the Old Covenant. Jesus through the dispensation of grace and the formation of the New Covenant offered unbridled freedom from the bondage of the Old Covenant

So what happens after this? They decided to write an epistle. **I believe this is the single most important epistle, or letter of the New Covenant.** Without understanding the Jerusalem Council, you will ponder back and forth concerning how the New Covenant affects Jews, Messianic Jews, Gentiles and Gentile Christians alike. The age old tug of war would still be raging. The Messianic Jews would try to pull Gentiles to the Old Covenant. The Gentile Christians would try to pull the Messianic Jews to the New Covenant. This is what I see in the church over the past 2,000 years. Jews, Messianic Jews, Gentiles, and Gentile Christians are struggling to discover how they are to rightly divide the Word of Truth. Jews migrate and see "things" from their side of the Old

Covenant. As soon as a Jew becomes Messianic they head right back to viewing the "things" of the Old Covenant and their position according to that Old Covenant. Doctrines such as Circumcision, observing the Torah, keeping the Commandments of Moses become a priority. It is just the way a Jew or Messianic Jew would think, it is all they have been taught. Actually, it was their rightful and legal way of observing the covenant that God made with the Jewish people. Now, when a Gentile becomes saved under the New Covenant they realize they are a sinner and they need a Savior. They accept Jesus, read the gospels, and learn about redemption by faith. We are saved by grace through faith; it is a gift of God not of works lest any man should boast Ephesians 2:8&9. I hope you can begin to see the struggle that really exists here regarding how to rightly divide the Word of Truth.

In the early church all they knew was the Old Testament, Circumcision, the Mosaic Law, and nothing else. Things are about to change at the Jerusalem Council, and four decrees are to be established.

Decree | Definition of Decree by Merriam-Webster
1: an order having the force of law by judicial decree. 2: a judicial decision especially in an equity or probate court broadly: judgment divorce decree interlocutory decree.

- **By definition, "A decree is an official order issued by a legal authority. Synonyms are listed here: order, edict a command, or a commandment, a proclamation."**

Acts 15:18; "Known to God from all eternity are all His works. Therefore I judge that we should not trouble those who are turning those who are from among the Gentiles who are turning to God, but that we write to them to abstain from things polluted by idols, from sexual immorality, from things strangled, and from blood." Four distinct decrees were decided on by the Holy Spirit for Gentile believers to follow. Honestly I have been saved for 45 years now. I have been

The Jerusalem Council Decision And Decrees Regarding Jew And Gentile

studying the four decrees for the past 25-30 years trying to understand what they really mean. In these past 25-30 years I am amazed at how many people never even heard of the four decrees!

1. **Abstain from things contaminated by idols;**
   Webster's definition of an idol (1: an object of extreme devotion a movie **idol** also: ideal sense 2: a representation or symbol of an object of worship broadly: a false god. 3a: a likeness of something. b obsolete: pretender, impostor.)
2. **Abstain from fornication; Webster's Definition of fornication.** : Consensual (see consensual sense 2) sexual intercourse between two persons not married to each other — compare adultery.
3. **Things strangled;**
   Webster's Definition of 1a: to **choke** to death by compressing the throat with something (such as a hand or rope): throttle. B: to obstruct seriously or fatally the normal breathing of. C: stifle. Aug 7, 2019
4. **From blood;**
   Webster's Definition (Entry 1 of 2) 1a(1) : the fluid that circulates in the heart, arteries, capillaries, and veins of a vertebrate animal carrying nourishment and oxygen to and bringing away waste products from all parts of the body. 2: the shedding of blood *also*: the taking of life

Right now you are thinking what do these four decrees really mean. It is important to put yourself in the mind set of that time. As we have discussed all they had was the Old Covenant at that time. The Covenant was made between God and the children of Abraham. The Gentiles were not a part of that covenant. Now after Peters Great sheet revelation, and the meeting at Cornelius house, Gentiles were obviously a part of the family of God. The question that remains here is what were the Jews and Messianic Jews to do with the Gentiles? Just think the Jerusalem Council consisted of the Apostles that Jesus handpicked and trained as well as the church at Jerusalem. But it was the Holy Spirit Himself who decided on the four decrees for "Gentiles" to follow. This was the most important decision in church history and today there are few that really understands what the decrees mean. To abstain from things offered to idols and fornication is self explanatory as described by their definitions. Gentile pagans were always committing idolatry, and eating things sacrificed to idols. Fornication covers pornography and all other sexual sins outside marriage. The other two decrees are not as simple. Following are two points of view concerning the other two decrees.

*To abstain from blood would mean that the Gentiles could not and should not participate in the Old Covenant rituals and Temple services. This is extremely important to understand when viewing this decree in this perspective. This would immediately eliminate Gentiles from all sacrifices and offerings of the Old Covenant. This is exactly why the four decrees and the New Covenant was established. The Old Covenant did not pertain to Gentiles. The Old Covenant was based on the shedding of blood. This could also pertain to the very act of circumcision the sign of the Old Covenant for the Jewish people. Pagans also drink blood in their religious services. The shedding of blood as defined could actually mean murder also.

*Abstain from things strangled. Once again this decree commands Gentiles not to live like other pagans who would strangle animals to keep the blood for consumption. Wikipedia, the Torah (Deut. 12:21) states that sheep and cattle should be slaughtered "as I have instructed you", but nowhere in the Five books of Moses are any of the practices of *shechita* described.[1] Instead, they have been handed down in Judaism's traditional Oral Torah, and codified in halakha. This ritual was passed down through the traditions of men. **Deuteronomy 21:12**, "If the place which the LORD thy God shall choose to put His name there be too far from thee, then thou shalt kill of thy herd and of thy flock, which the LORD hath given thee, as I have commanded thee, and thou shalt eat within thy gates, after all the desire of thy soul."

These four decrees were laid out to give the Gentiles a necessary fundamental foundation of things to abstain from. Those Gentiles who accepted Jesus Christ were not to live like other Gentiles.

So these decrees were the answer to these questions.

1. **Were Gentile believers supposed to circumcise their children?**
2. **Were Gentiles to observe the Law of Moses?**

Many believe the answer would be a simple yes, but it was not. They think Gentiles should circumcise their children as a religious ritual rite in Judaism, and they should command their children to observe the Laws of Moses.

7.
The Jerusalem Councils Letter/Epistle

To avoid any further disagreements concerning these issues regarding Gentiles they put the decisions of the Jerusalem Council and the four decrees in the form of a letter. This was an epistle that was written by the apostles and elders who had been divinely directed and taught by the resurrected Messiah Jesus Christ. Please note at the Jerusalem Council these New Covenant Commandments, decrees were Divinely decided on by the Holy Spirit Himself, and were delivered by the Jewish apostles and elders in Jerusalem for the Gentiles to observe (Acts 15:28).

Please remember this letter was the answer to these two main questions.

1. **Were Gentile believers supposed to circumcise their children?**
2. **Were Gentiles to observe the Law of Moses?**

As we go through Paul's journeys we will look specifically at how these two questions were answered by the Jerusalem council letter.

Acts 15:23-29 they wrote this letter;
"The apostles, the elders, and the brethren, to the brethren who are of the Gentiles in Antioch, Syria, and Cecilia;

Greetings,

Since we have heard that some who went out from us have troubled you with their words, unsettling your souls saying, "you must be circumcised and you must keep the law- to whom we gave no such commandments- it seemed good to us, being assembled with one accord, to chose certain men to send to you with our beloved Barnabus and Paul, men who have risked their lives for the name of our Lord Jesus Christ. We have therefore sent Judas and Silas, who will also report the same things by word of mouth. **For it seemed good to the Holy Spirit, and to us, to lay on you no greater burden than these necessary things**, that you abstain from things contaminated by idols, sexual immorality, things strangled and blood. If you keep yourself free from these things you will do well. Farewell." Why was the letter even written if there was no change in the covenant? If the entire Old Covenant stayed the same and Gentiles were suppose to convert to Judaism they would not have decided to write this letter.

At the Jerusalem Council Four specific decrees, commandments, and laws were decided on by the Holy Spirit from which Gentiles were to abstain from.

Decree | Definition of Decree by Merriam-Webster

1: an order having the force of law by judicial decree. 2: a judicial decision especially in an equity or probate court broadly: judgment divorce decree interlocutory decree.

- **By definition, "A decree is an official order issued by a legal authority. Synonyms are listed here: order, edict a command, or a commandment, a proclamation."**

These decrees were put into an epistle/letter and delivered to the Gentile believers. **Acts 15:36** "then after some days Paul said to Barnabus let us now go back to our brethren **in every city** where we have preached the Word of the Lord and see how they are doing." Paul and Barnabus had a disagreement on who was going with them. **Important fact here is that Paul and Barnabus separate here and Paul decides to take Timothy with him. Acts 16:3**, "Paul wanted Timothy to go with him. He took him and circumcised him because of the Jews in that region, for they all knew his father was a Greek, but his mother was a Jew." Being a Jew was determined from the mother, not the fathers. **Acts 16:4, "as they went through the cities they delivered the decrees for them to keep, which were determined by the (Holy Spirit) apostles and elders in Jerusalem."** A very important revelation of the New Covenant happens here. Paul and Timothy deliver the decrees to every city. What cities did they deliver these decrees, commandments, and laws? **After the Jerusalem Council you will see they traveled and delivered these four decrees to Galatia, Philippi, Thessalonians, Corinth, Ephesus and Rome.** In each city, we will observe that as they ministered to Jews and Gentiles alike, they grew the church, and specifically advised how the Gentiles were to view circumcision, the law, and the observance of the Old Covenant. These are the primary issues as well as the necessary questions they strove to define and answer at the Jerusalem Council. You will also see that the four decrees are mentioned throughout the New Covenant Epistles as well as the book of the Revelation of Jesus Christ. Each epistle that was written later describes in detail how the Gentiles were to view these issues regarding believers in the Jewish Messiah, Jesus Christ. Many try to minimize the importance of the Jerusalem Council. Those who try to minimize the importance of this Council do not see the entire revelation that lies behind it. This Council was and is the most important Council in the History of the World. It is the letter/epistle that lays out what the Gentiles are to do under the New Covenant. It also tells the Messianic Jews how they are to deal with Gentile believers in the Messiah. This letter/epistle was delivered to the cities that Paul had visited. These were Gentile believers in the Messiah. Through the rest of the New Covenant, Gentiles are given instructions on how they are to live in a manner worthy of their calling.

8.
Galatians Receive the Jerusalem Councils decisions (Acts 16:6)

T he first Gentile church where Paul and Timothy delivered the Jerusalem Council letter was in the Galatia region. I would like to start this chapter quoting these extremely important scriptures. This is how the Lord revealed this mystery to me, please be mindful and remember this. **Ephesians 3:3** "by referring to this when you read, you can understand my insight into the mystery of Christ. **Which for generations has been hidden**, but now it has been revealed to the holy apostles and prophets, to be specific the **Gentiles are fellow citizens and are of the house of the Lord.**"

The Jerusalem Councils decisions: Acts 15:23-29 they wrote this letter by them;
"The apostles, the elders, and the brethren, to the brethren who are of the Gentiles in Antioch, Syria, and Cecilia;

Greetings,
    Since we have heard that some who went out from us have troubled you with their words, unsettling your souls saying, "**you must be circumcised and you must keep the law- to whom we gave no such commandments**- it seemed good to us, being assembled with one accord, to chose certain men to send to you with our beloved Barnabus and Paul,

men who have risked their lives for the name of our Lord Jesus Christ. We have therefore sent Judas and Silas, who will also report the same things by word of mouth. **For it seemed good to the Holy Spirit, and to us, to lay on you no greater burden than these necessary things**, that you abstain from things contaminated by idols, sexual immorality, things strangled and blood. If you keep yourself free from these things you will do well. Farewell."

Were these exact issues and decrees dealt with in the writings of the New Covenant? Were these specific issues mentioned in the Epistle that was written later to the Gentile churches? Throughout the rest of this book I will show that the decisions and decrees that the Holy Spirit made during the Jerusalem Council are found in every epistle that was delivered to the Gentile churches. **The Jerusalem Council made decisions and decrees regarding circumcision, the law, fornication (sexual immorality), idolatry, things strangled and blood.** Remember these decrees were established to answer the two very important questions that were addressed at the Jerusalem Council.

1. **Were Gentile believers supposed to circumcise their children?**
2. **Were Gentiles to observe the Law of Moses?**

Galatians 1:6-8, "I marvel that you are turning away so soon from Him who called you into the gospel of Christ (New Covenant) for another Gospel (Old Covenant) which is really not another gospel, but there are some who trouble you and want to pervert the **Gospel of Christ** (New Covenant). But even if we or an angel from heaven preach another gospel to you than that what we have preached let him be accursed." These are extremely important and powerful words coming from the apostle Paul and Timothy to the church at Galatia. This letter to the Galatians was written and delivered after they delivered the Jerusalem Council letter. You will see here the same word troubling which was again found in the Jerusalem council letter. **Acts 15:24, "since we have heard that some from us have gone out and**

Galatians Receive The Jerusalem Councils Decisions (Acts 16:6)

troubled you with their words..." This troubling was concerning the Old Covenants views on **Circumcision** and the Laws of Moses. These two specific issues were discussed during the Jerusalem Council. **Galatians 2:7,** "When they saw the gospel for the **uncircumcised** (New Covenant/ Gentiles) had been entrusted to me, as the gospel for the **circumcision** (Old Covenant / Jewish) was to Peter." Here we see two gospels mentioned, two apostles, to two different groups of people. **Galatians 2:8,** "for He who worked effectually for Peter in his apostleship to the **circumcised** also worked effectually for me in the **uncircumcised**. **Galatians 2:9,** "when James, Cephas, and John, who seemed to be pillars." This is relating back specifically to the Jerusalem Council meeting in **Acts 15:13** James answered, **Acts 15:14** Simon (Peter). **Two specific Apostles; Peter and Paul, representing two completely different groups of people uncircumcised Gentiles and circumcised Jews viewing two different covenants.** I know many people initially say well there is one new man in Christ. I agree, but that is a partial truth. If it were just one new man, and there were no questions regarding Jew, Messianic Jew, Gentile and Gentile Christians, the Covenants, circumcision, or the law there would be no need for another Covenant, and we would not be having this discussion. There is one new man, but how is that new man to regard his personal position under the New Covenant. An egg or a peach is one whole, but each has three parts. A husband and wife are one but they are two different people. How do all of these different parts (Old Covenant, New Covenant, Jews, Messianic Jews, Gentiles, Gentile Christians, circumcision, uncircumcision, the Law, and the four decrees) function in one body of the one new man in the New Covenant? **Galatians 2:11,** "Now when Peter came to Antioch I withstood him to his face, for prior to men coming down from James he use to eat with the Gentiles; but when they came he withdrew and separated himself, fearing those who were of the **circumcision** (Jews and Messianic Jews), and the rest of the Jews with him played in their hypocrisy." **Circumcised** Jews were not permitted to associate/eat with **uncircumcised** Gentiles. Peter who received the Great Sheet Revelation

(**Acts 10**) began to eat with **uncircumcised** Gentile men, but when the **circumcised** Jews heard of this and went to meet Peter, he immediately withdrew from the **uncircumcised** Gentiles. Paul rebuked him for this hypocrisy. **Galatians 2:14,** "but when I heard they were not straightforward about the gospel (New Covenant), I said to Peter before them all, if you being a Jew live in the manner of the Gentiles and not like the Jews, why do you compel Gentiles to live as Jews." Peter was still struggling, or battling the same tug of war with these issues regarding Jew, Messianic Jew, and Gentile and Gentile Christians believers in the Messiah. The apostles were still learning, themselves, how to deal with the Truth regarding the Jerusalem Council and the decisions the Holy Spirit made. So we clearly see here they were dealing with the decisions of the Jerusalem Council. I highlighted **circumcision** and **uncircumcision** just so you see the importance of it just in this chapter.

- What does this say about the Laws of Moses discussed during the Jerusalem Council?
- Was the law also a part of the epistle written later to those at Galatia? If they were to keep the Mosaic Law as some say, why is there such an issue about the law?
- Why was there a Jerusalem Council?
- Why was there a need for another covenant if there were no changes to the Old Covenant?

If the Gentiles were to become Jews in order to be saved then no issues at all would have needed to be addressed. **Galatians 3:1-4,** "oh you foolish Galatians who has bewitched you that you should not obey the truth.....? Did you receive the Spirit by the works of the Law, or by hearing and Faith? Having begun by the Spirit are you now perfected by the flesh? He who supplies miracles among you, does He do it by the works of the Law or hearing and of faith." **Galatians 3:8** .... "God would justify the Gentiles by faith." **Galatians 3:10,** "those who are under the Law are under a curse;" **Galatians 3:13,** "Christ redeemed us from the curse of the law." **Galatians 3:17,** "the law that came 430 years later does not nullify a promise previously ratified by God as to nullify the Covenant." So you can clearly see here that these same issues discussed at the Jerusalem Council were still being discussed by the apostles and prophets concerning Jews, Messianic Jews, Gentiles, and Gentile Christians. How were they to honor these decisions that were made at the Jerusalem Council? The Jerusalem Councils, four decrees were put into a form of a letter (**Acts 16:1-4**) and were delivered to the Gentile churches. They had to make these necessary decisions regarding Jews, Messianic Jews, Gentiles, and Gentile Christians and how they were to view the Covenants of God. That was the sole purpose the Jerusalem Council. They did not know what to do with the New Covenant believers in the Messiah. Obviously, Gentiles were different than the Jewish and Messianic Jewish believers. In the days and times of Jesus all they had was the Old Covenant and what it meant to the Jews. Then the Messianic Jews and Gentile Christians believed and received the Holy Spirit. It will be the same way at the second coming, but reversed. There will be primarily Gentile believers and we will be deciding how the Jews will be received. By now you know how strongly I believe in the period and process of restoration in the Kingdom of God. **Here is another example of restoration that will be fulfilled**. In the beginning Jews believed, then Messianic Jews believed in the Messiah, then Gentiles believed. In the later days of the church Gentiles believe in the Messiah. We are now seeing the Messianic Jews believe, and then finally all Jews will believe when the Messiah returns to rule at Jerusalem. Why? Israel was not a nation until 1948. Through one thousand nine hundred forty eight years, there were hardly any Messianic Jews on the earth. Today because the restoration of all things is taking place, we have more Messianic Jews than ever before. It has only been a period 70 years since Israel became a nation, and we can see the impact of Messianic Jews coming into the Body of Christ. Just as the Gentiles came into the faith, so at the restoration of all things the Messianic Jews will be restored back into the Faith. The Gentiles are being challenged regarding the feasts, holy days or holidays, the laws of Moses, the Torah, and the writing of the Old Covenant. How are they (the Jews and Messianic Jews) to regard the New Covenant? This is exactly what the Gentiles had to do in the beginning regarding the New Covenant and the Jerusalem Council. It is clearly the process and period of the restoration of all things that is taking place.

Importance of Messianic Jewish Movement: There were very few Messianic Jews before 1948, as recently as 2018; there are many Messianic Jews who are having an impact on today's church. It was seventy years from Jesus' birth to the destruction of the temple in 70 A.D., and we have 70 years from the birth of Israel as a nation to 2018 when the United States recognized Jerusalem as Israel's capital and placed our embassy there. Gentile Christian believers are now being challenged by Messianic Jews about their stance on the New Covenant regarding the feast days, Sabbath days, Mosaic Laws, the Torah, and the Old Covenant. Finally, let's take a closer look at Galatians 5 regarding the Jerusalem Council and the letter that was written and delivered to these churches. Galatians chapter 2 discussed **circumcision** and its importance. **Circumcision** was the sign of the Jews in the Old Covenant. If you were not **circumcised** on the eighth day according to the law, that person was to be cut off from their people (put to death/ often stoned). This was the eternal everlasting covenant that the Lord God Jehovah made with Abraham. **Galatians 5:1-4**, "stand fast therefore in the liberty by which Christ has made us free, and do not be entangled again with a yoke of bondage. Indeed **I Paul say to you that if you become circumcised Christ will profit you nothing**." And I testify again to everyman that is **circumcised**, that he is a debtor to keep the whole law." Can you imagine the ramifications of these words to the Jewish believers and all those that knew the Old Covenant? Please remember that was all they had at that time, because the New Covenant was not finalized. So they knew the promises of the Old Covenant; the promises that were made to Abraham were an everlasting eternal covenant. The word of Paul would have seemed to the Jews as heresy, but in reality they

Galatians Receive The Jerusalem Councils Decisions (Acts 16:6)

were proclamations of the Jerusalem Council and the New Covenant. **The Jews and Messianic Jews knew the importance of circumcision.** They were in the wilderness for forty years because they did not **circumcise** their children. See many do not realize this truth. **Joshua 5:4,** states this is the reason Joshua **circumcised** them "For all the people who had come out had been **circumcised**, but all the people born in the wilderness, on the way as they came out of Egypt, had not been **circumcised**." For the children of Israel walked in the wilderness forty years till all the people who were men of war were consumed. **This happened because they did not obey the voice of the Lord regarding circumcision. The reason they had to stay in the wilderness is that the men of war did not circumcise their children.** Now think how powerful these words were that Paul was stating that **circumcision means nothing**. **Circumcision** or **uncircumcision** means nothing but a brand new man in Christ.

This holds true today as we see the struggle between Jew, Messianic Jew, Gentile and Gentile Christians, and both Old and New Covenants. If they were to go strictly by the Old Covenant, the Jews would have killed Paul because of what he was preaching regarding **circumcision** and the law. **Joshua 5:8,** "So it was that when they had finished **circumcising** all the people that they stayed in their places in the camp until they were all healed." Every single one who was not **circumcised** and who came out of Egypt had to be **circumcised**. This is one of the many reasons why the Messianic Jews were saying at the Jerusalem Council that the Gentiles who believed in the Messiah had to be **circumcised**. They also argued that Gentiles had to observe the Laws of Moses; but the Jerusalem Council decided this was NOT true for Gentile believers. They made the decision with the Holy Spirit and determined the four decrees or laws, put it in the form of the letter, and delivered it to all the cities. **The Jerusalem Council made decisions and decrees regarding circumcision, the law, fornication (sexual immorality), idolatry, things strangled and blood.**

9.

Philippians Receive the Jerusalem Councils decisions (Acts 16)

Acts 16:12 shows the next city they traveled to was Philippi to discuss what the Jerusalem council had decided. Remember the question debated in Acts 15:5, "But some of the sect of the Pharisees who had believed rose up saying it is necessary to circumcise them (Gentiles) and command them (Gentiles) to keep the laws of Moses." The letter wrote and all epistles that follow addressed this issue and decided it was not necessary for the Gentiles.

*E*phesians 3:3," by referring to this when you read, you can understand my insight into the mystery of Christ. Which for generations has been hidden, but now it has been revealed to the holy apostles and prophets, to be specific the **Gentiles are fellow citizens and are of the house of the Lord.**"

* Acts 15:23-29 they wrote this letter by them;

The Jerusalem Councils decisions: **Acts 15:23-29** they wrote this letter by them;
"The apostles, the elders, and the brethren, to the brethren who are of the Gentiles in Antioch, Syria, and Cecilia;

Greetings,

Since we have heard that some who went out from us have troubled you with their words, unsettling your souls saying, "**you must be circumcised and you must keep the law- to whom we gave no such commandments**- it seemed good to us, being assembled with one accord, to chose certain men to send to you with our beloved Barnabus and Paul, men who have risked their lives for the name of our Lord Jesus Christ. We have therefore sent Judas and Silas, who will also report the same things by word of mouth. **For it seemed good to the Holy Spirit, and to us, to lay on you no greater burden than these necessary things**, that you abstain from things contaminated by idols, sexual immorality, things strangled and blood. If you keep yourself free from these things you will do well. Farewell."

Now let's take a closer look at the epistle written to those Gentiles who were at Philippi and see if Paul addresses the Jerusalem Council letter and the decrees that were decided on for the Gentiles to follow. Could he possibly mention circumcision again? I promise I will not highlight it all through this epistle, but I just want you to see the importance of the issue of circumcision and the law that was mentioned in the Jerusalem Council.

Philippians 3:2, "beware of dogs beware of evil workers; beware of the mutilation (**the circumcision**)! For we (Gentiles) are the true circumcision, who worship God in the Spirit, rejoices in Jesus Christ, and have no confidence in the flesh; though I might also have confidence in the flesh." Here again Paul is addressing a Gentile church in Philippi regarding the Jerusalem Council and the decrees that were decided on for the Gentiles to follow. **The main issue of the epistle to those at Philippi was circumcision.** According to Paul who is the true circumcision? Paul is saying the Gentile Christians and Messianic Jews, who accept Christ, worship, God, and put no confidence in the flesh are the true circumcision (or New Covenant). The Jews and the Jewish believers in the Messiah only had the Old Covenant to go by at that time. Therefore according to the Jew's Old Covenant, Paul was wrong by saying Gentiles were the true circumcision; the Gentiles did not circumcise their children according to the customs of Moses nor follow the laws of Moses. Thank God for the New Covenant. As we have discussed, In Joshua 5:4 circumcision was the main sign of the covenant between God and Abraham. Paul was standing firm on the Jerusalem Council's decisions (Acts 15:18-29) regarding the Gentile believers in Christ. **Philippians 3:4-6**, "though I might have confidence in the flesh. If anyone think he may have confidence in the flesh, I more so: circumcised the eight day, of the stock of Israel, of the tribe of Benjamin, a Hebrew of Hebrews, concerning the law, a Pharisee; concerning zeal a persecutor of the church, concerning righteousness which is found in the law, blameless. But what things was gain to me, I have counted loss for the sake of Christ."

What a powerful statement and everything an Old Covenant Jew like Paul desired to be. He was making a declaration that he was counting them all as dung, loss for the Christ. Paul was proclaiming to all the Jews salvation was now through Christ, **not circumcision and the law**. Paul gives a detailed description of all his accomplishments being a Jew and declares them as loss for Christ. **Philippians 3:8-9**, "yet indeed I count all thing loss for the excellence of the knowledge of Christ Jesus my Lord, for whom I have suffered the loss of all things, and count them as rubbish, that I might gain Christ and be found in Him not having a righteousness of my own, which is from the law, but that which is through faith in Jesus Christ". **Do we need to be circumcised and keep the Mosaic Law to be saved?**

What amazes me is that when someone says we are not under the law, or we do not need to keep the laws of Moses to be saved- I have witnessed, time and again, the attack that immediately follows. Paul gave it up and people today still try to migrate back to it, they desire to be enslaved to a Law they cannot keep. People tend to protect the Mosaic Law. The fact is no one can keep it; no one has ever fulfilled the law except Jesus Christ. Even nonbelievers get angry, they want to be under a law that they cannot keep. Isn't that interesting- Gentile non believers get mad when someone says we are not under the Law of Moses? We have been set free from the Law of Moses, that is the truth, we are under a New Covenant. Paul was divinely chosen of God to be an apostle to the Gentile people.

Paul fully understood the Old Covenant, circumcision, and the law. God called Paul to write two thirds of the New Covenant, attend the first Jerusalem Council, and deliver the letter to the Gentile churches.

10.
Thessalonians Receive the Jerusalem Councils decisions (Acts 17)

After Paul left Philippi he headed to Thessalonia. **1 Thessalonians 2:2** "but even after we had been mistreated at Philippi (Acts 16:12), as you know, we were bold in our God to speak to you the gospel of God in much affliction." You will continue to see the same pattern throughout the book of Acts each chapter represents a city Paul and Timothy visited in order to deliver the letter from the Jerusalem Council. These were Gentile believers and this was a New Covenant to them. The Gentiles did not know if they were to go back and convert to Judaism. **Acts 15:5, "But some of the sect of the Pharisees who had believed rose up saying it is necessary to circumcise them (Gentiles) and command them (Gentiles) to keep the laws of Moses."**

- Remember the four decrees were established to answer these two very important questions that were addressed at the Jerusalem Council.

3. Were Gentile believers supposed to circumcise their children?
4. Were Gentiles to observe the Law of Moses?

Paul was establishing the New Covenant based on faith in Christ first, the Jerusalem Council and their decisions. Look in the first chapter and see how Paul immediately refers back to their visitation in Acts, **1 Thessalonians 1:9**, "for they themselves declare concerning us what manner of entry we had with you, and how you **turned from idols** to serve the living and true God, and to wait for His Son from heaven, whom He raised from the dead, even Jesus." Once again holding true to the revelation pattern we set forth. Paul addresses one of the decrees (abstain from things offered to idols) that was established at the Jerusalem Council for Gentiles to follow. **1 Thessalonians 2:1** also solidifies this point of view. "For you yourselves know brethren, that our coming to you was not in vain. But after we had been mistreated in Philippi, as you know, we were bold in God to speak the truth amid much opposition." This is exactly what happened in **Acts 16:11-40** when they were delivering the decrees they had decided on at the Jerusalem Council. The Jerusalem council and the decisions they made were the reason they traveled through the cities. Was there any where else in this epistle to the Thessalonians that Paul mentions one of the decrees determined at the Jerusalem Council? **1 Thessalonians 4:2** reads for you know **what commandments (decrees)** we gave you through our Lord Jesus Christ. Is there any scriptural support to show that Paul delivered any commandments to the Gentile Church at Thessalonians? I say there most definitely is. You must know the pattern to see the revelation. The Jerusalem council was held in **Acts 15**, the Holy Spirit decided on the decrees **Acts 15:23**, the letter from the Jerusalem Council was written **Acts 15:18-23**. The letter written at the Jerusalem Council was delivered to each city **Acts 16:5. Acts 17:1** they delivered the Jerusalem letter to the church at Thessalonians.

The letter consisted of the four decrees or commandments. These were four commandments divinely given from the Holy Spirit for Gentile believers in the Messiah to observe and follow. So will we see in the letter of 1 Thessalonians any of the decrees, commandments mentioned? Remember the dictionary definition of a decree: **"A decree is**

Thessalonians Receive The Jerusalem Councils Decisions (acts 17)

an official order issued by a legal authority. **Synonyms: Order, edict a command or a commandment, a proclamation.**

1 Thessalonians 4:3, "for this is the will of God, your sanctification: that you should **abstain from sexual immorality**, that each one of you should know how to possess your vessel in sanctification and honor, not in the passion of lust, like the other Gentiles who do not know God." Paul immediately refers to one of the four decrees that were decided on at the Jerusalem Council. He could have spoken of anything regarding commandments and how they were to walk in sanctification. Sexual immorality and fornication were not specifically mentioned in the Ten Commandments. Remember all they had at that time to read was the Old Covenant, the torah, the laws of Moses. Paul does not specifically mention any of the Old Covenant Law, instead he purposely directs the Gentiles to one of the four decrees, and commandments that the Holy Spirit decided on in **Acts 15:28-29**.

11.

Corinthians Receive the Jerusalem Councils decisions (Acts 18)

ACTS 18:1, "**After these things Paul departed from Athens and went to Corinth**". Paul and Timothy traveled to Corinth to deliver the decrees that were decided on at the Jerusalem Council for Gentile believers in Christ to follow (Acts 16:1-5). Did they speak specifically about the Jerusalem Council and decrees in this epistle to those at Corinth? First of all, in **1 Corinthians 3:1** Paul establishes an important thought, "I could not speak to you as spiritual people, but as to carnal, as to babes in Christ. I fed you with milk, not solid food, for not even now are you able to receive it". Did they stray from the decisions and decrees decided on at the Jerusalem Council? Could Paul possibly be speaking in reference to the decisions that were made at the Jerusalem Council? Were any of the four decrees from the Jerusalem Council, ever spoken about or referenced to in the epistle to those at Corinth? **I say that reference to the Jerusalem Council is found in every epistle of the New Covenant**. The Jerusalem Councils, decisions, decrees, and letter were the mere foundation of the New Covenant for Gentiles to observe and follow. By now you understand the Jerusalem Council and its importance. Let's see if Paul referred to the Jerusalem Council when he addressed the Corinthians. **The Jerusalem Council made decisions and four decrees regarding fornication (sexual immorality), idolatry, things strangled and blood.**

- Remember these decrees were established to answer the two very important questions that were addressed at the Jerusalem Council.

1. **Were Gentile believers supposed to circumcise their children?**
2. **Were Gentiles to observe the Law of Moses?**

1 Corinthians 5:1: "It is actually reported that there is sexual immorality (pornea) among you, and such sexual immorality that is even named among the Gentiles- that a man has his father's wife! And you are puffed up, and have not rather mourned". So immediately, right at the beginning of this epistle Paul specifically addresses one of the four decrees (fornication/ pornea) from the Jerusalem Council. Fornication is absolutely one of the four decrees. In **1 Corinthians 5:5**, he said to deliver such a person over to Satan for the destruction of his flesh so that his spirit might be saved. Also take a look at **1 Corinthians 5:7-8**, where he told them Christ our Passover was sacrificed for us; **therefore, let us keep the feast**, not with old leaven, nor with the leaven of malice and wickedness, but with the unleavened bread of sincerity and truth. I am not going to state my understanding and views on the feasts, but you can see that Paul tells them to keep the Feast of Passover. In the first few chapters I addressed this showing how we, as Gentiles view the feasts from a different point of view than the Jews and Messianic Jews. Christ is our Passover; He was and is the fulfillment of that feast. I believe as a Gentile that we observe Passover by celebrating Jesus and the Last Supper, not by trying to do the feast itself. That is impossible to do since the Temple is destroyed. With no Temple you cannot physically fulfill the feasts, but we can observe and honor them in Christ. In this case, the Jews would be looking at the Passover, and how God delivered the Jews out of Egypt. Many Jews and Messianic Jews still do this today. We, as New Testament Gentile Christians see the Feast of Passover differently. The Jews celebrated the Feast of Passover for 1500 years and when the Passover Lamb of God came they crucified

Him! Remember same glass half full, or half empty? **Every one of these groups could see the same glass half full, or half empty. They see the same glass, same amount of water, but come to different conclusions. What I mean by this is they can see the same scriptures but interpret them differently, and come to different conclusions according to what group they come out of.** Hopefully you honor and celebrate the Feast of Passover realizing Jesus died for our sins. Four totally different views of the same Passover feast show how the Old Covenant applied to the Jews differently than the Gentiles. The New Covenant applies to the Messianic Jews and Gentile Christians differently than the Jews. People accept the difference in how the Old Covenant applies but do not yet fully see or understand that this same principle applies to the New Covenant. In **1 Corinthians 7:18-19** it says Paul then immediately goes and addresses another one of the decrees or issues that were dealt with at the Jerusalem Council, **circumcision!** Was anyone called while circumcised? Let him not become uncircumcised. "**Was anyone called while not uncircumcised let him NOT become circumcised?** Circumcision is nothing and uncircumcision is nothing, but the keeping of the commandments of God is what is important." I say we must consider that Paul was speaking of the Jerusalem Council's four decrees as the commandments of God, not the Ten Commandments or laws of Moses. Could you imagine the impact that these words had on those who heard them? **Paul said circumcision was nothing!** At this time all they knew was circumcision! The only writing they had to guide them was from the Torah. If any man was not circumcised they were to be cut off from the Jewish people. **Genesis 17:10-14 "this is my covenant which you shall keep, between me and you and your descendents after you. Every male child among you must be circumcised.... It will be a sign of the Covenant between Me and you. Every male child among you is to be circumcised on the eighth day."** Obviously the Jerusalem Councils decisions and the decrees that were decided on by the Holy Spirit, apostles, and elders changed this view of circumcision. **Acts 15:1**:"certain men came down from Judea and taught the brethren unless you are circumcised according to the customs of Moses you cannot be saved." Circumcision and the observance of the Mosaic Law were the reason the Jerusalem Council had to be held. The Messianic Jewish apostles and elders had to make a decision regarding the New Covenant and Gentile believers. Were Gentiles to circumcise their children according to the customs of Moses and were they to be taught to observe the laws of Moses? **The Jerusalem Council made the decision, and the answer was No. The Holy Spirit of God directed the apostles and elders at the Jerusalem Council, the decisions were made, they were put in the form of a letter, and this letter or epistle was delivered to the New Covenant churches.**

1 Corinthians 8:1: "Now concerning the things offered to idols." Paul is going to address another one of the four decrees or commandments of God that was decided on at the Jerusalem Council. The 4 decrees that the Jerusalem Council decided on encompassed many of the Ten Commandments in the Old Covenant. Let me give you an example of just two of the Ten Commandments and how they are similar to the decrees in the New Covenant. The first two of the 10 commandments were in reference idols. **Exodus 20:3** the first commandment states "you shall have no other Gods before Me". **Exodus 20:4** states "you shall not make for yourself any graven image-any likeness of anything that is in heaven above, or that is in the earth beneath, or that is in the water under the earth." **1 Corinthians 8:4** states, "therefore concerning the eating of things offered to idols, we know that an idol is nothing in the world, and there is no God but one." He will address this decree or commandment and explain how these New Covenant Gentiles were to walk in obedience to these decrees or commandments of God. As we have seen and will continue to see the four decrees or the four Commandments of God are the reason and underlying current why all of the epistles were written to the Gentile churches. **Paul as an apostle of God was establishing the New Covenant based on the Jerusalem Council and the decisions that were made by the Holy Spirit for Gentiles to follow.** The Gentiles, as a people, were known to be pagans. Gentiles worshipped idols and ate food that was offered to idols. This is also where the abstaining from blood comes from. Blood is known to be a major part of all pagan sacrifices and idol worship. The Gentiles were no longer to sacrifice animals for the forgiveness of their sins; therefore, they need to abstain from the shedding of the blood of the animal sacrifice. The Old Covenant was based on animal sacrifice and the shedding of blood. For Gentiles to abstain from the shedding of blood they could not participate in any of the animal sacrifices of the Old Covenant. Abstain from the shedding of blood could also mean they were to abstain from circumcision as a rite to become a Jew. Blood was shed obviously at the ritual of circumcision. Also in **1 Corinthians 9:1** Paul cries out, "Am I not and apostle?" He had been chosen by God for a specific purpose and function in order to bring salvation to the Gentile people. Yes, Paul was most definitely an apostle chosen by God, but because he was writing regarding the Jerusalem Council, the four decrees, and establishment of a New Covenant he was not accepted by men. Jews who followed the laws of Moses and Circumcision hated him. They felt he was preaching a Gospel contrary to the Old Covenant and the Law. For thousands of years circumcision and the Laws of Moses were all the Jews ever had, they were the fundamental foundation of the eternal everlasting covenant God made with Abraham. The Old Covenant was not written to Gentiles. In **1 Corinthians 10** Paul reminds them of circumstances and situations that occurred in the Old Covenant and how these should be examples for us NOT to follow. **1Corinthians 10:6,** "now these things became our examples, to the intent that we should not lust after evil things as they also lusted. And do not become Idolaters as were some of them..." **1Corinthians 10:8;** "nor let us commit sexual immorality, as some of them did, and in one day 23,000 fell; do not let us tempt Christ as some of them did and were destroyed by serpents." **1 Corinthians 10:11** states, "now all of these things happened to them as examples, and they were written for our admonition, upon which the end of the age has come." Paul focuses here on idolatry, and fornication, two of the

4 decrees on which the Jerusalem Council decided on. **1 Corinthians 10:14 states,** "therefore, my beloved, **flee from idolatry.**"

Before I saw the importance and revelation of the Jerusalem Council, I knew we were not to worship idols. I remember thinking that if this is so very important and it was such an issue in the past, then how is this affecting us today? I am seriously questioning what some of the modern day idols are. What could we possibly be worshipping in ignorance? Throughout the entire Old Covenant the Israelites fell into idolatry over and over again. They worshipped Ashtoreth, Ishtar, Tamuz, Nimrod, Semiramis, Ashtoreth poles, Astarte, and many other idols. Could Gentiles today be worshipping these same idols? I actually had to search to find who these false gods were. Could they possibly be a part of the modern day church in any way? I pray you would also be enlightened; please search the origins of Christmas, Easter, and Halloween. You may be surprised how they relate to idol worship today. After my research, I realized how much idolatry was an issue in today's church. I had to repent and turn away from worshipping the idols of this world.

In summary of the letter to those at Corinth we see in 1 Corinthians 3, Paul addressed the maturity of believers regarding the Jerusalem Council. Chapter 4 states "let a man consider us as servants of Christ and stewards of the mysteries of God." In chapter 5 Paul dealt specifically with sexual immorality one of the four decrees decided on at the Jerusalem Council. In chapter 6 Paul addresses how we are to judge within the church regarding these decrees. In chapter 8 Paul wrote concerning the things offered to idols and eating things offered to idols. In chapter 9 Paul addresses his position as an apostle relating to the Jerusalem Council and the decrees on which they decided. In 1 Corinthians 10 Paul shows how the things that happened to the Jews should not happen to us Gentiles. Gentile Christians should learn from the mistakes from the Jews in the Old Covenant. He specifically addressed idolatry, sexual immorality and how these decrees now relate to the Gentiles and their position in the New Covenant. 2 Corinthians also deals with the difference between the two Covenants and how we

Gentiles are to view the Old Covenant. These are pretty strong words concerning the Old Covenant but keep in mind what Paul said in the first letter to those at Corinth when he wrote **2 Corinthians 3:6:** "who also made us sufficient as ministers of the New Covenant, not of the letter (Old Covenant), but of the Spirit of the living God, not on tablets of stone but on tablets of flesh, that is of the heart." **2 Corinthians 3:7** states, "but if **the ministry of death** (the Old Covenant) written and engraved on stones, was glorious so that the children of Israel (Old Covenant) could not look steadily at the face of Moses because of the glory of his countenance, which glory was passing away, how will the ministry of the Spirit (New Covenant) not be more glorious? For if the ministry of condemnation had glory the ministry of righteousness exceeds much more in glory." **2 Corinthians 3:13:** "unlike Moses who put a veil over his face so that the children of Israel could not look steadily at the end of what was passing away (Old Covenant). But their minds were blinded. For until this same day the veil remains unlifted in the reading of the Old Covenant, because the veil is taken away in Christ. But even till this day when Moses is read the veil remains on their hearts."

This is exactly what I am saying regarding the Feast of the Old Covenant. They honored and worshipped them and when the Messiah came to fulfill them, they (the Jews) crucified Jesus. Their hearts and minds were blinded. Nevertheless, when one turns to the Lord the veil is taken away. **Paul was proclaiming these truths when all they had was the Old Covenant.** If the Old Covenant was done away with, the ministry of death was done away with. What was left for Gentiles to follow? Today we know the answer is the New Covenant. The Jerusalem Council was the pivot point of the entire New Covenant. This Council was when they made specific decisions regarding Gentiles and how they were to view the Old Covenant. As Paul was writing this epistle they had no New Covenant, and their letters were the New Covenant. Just think of the ramifications of these writings. People would be stoned just for transgressing the Sabbath Day. **Here Paul is proclaiming the**

Old Covenant written on stones (Ten Commandments) as the ministry of death.

12.

Ephesians Receive the Jerusalem Councils decisions (Acts 19)

***A**cts 19:1:* "...and it happened while Apollos was at Corinth (previous city), that Paul, having passed through the upper regions, came to Ephesus (to deliver the letter created at the first Jerusalem Council)."

- Remember the decrees were established to answer theses two very important questions that were addressed at the Jerusalem Council.

1. Were Gentile believers supposed to circumcise their children?
2. Were Gentiles to observe the Law of Moses?

Were these issues addressed in the letter to those at Ephesus?

Ephesians 2:11: "Therefore remember that you, once Gentiles in the flesh who are called uncircumcision by what is called the circumcision made in the flesh by human hands. That at that time you were aliens from the commonwealth of Israel and strangers from the covenant and promises. Having no hope and without God in this world. But now in Christ Jesus you who were once far off have been brought near by the blood of Christ." **Ephesians 2:14:** "For He himself is our peace , who has made both one, and has broken down the middle wall of separation, having abolished in His flesh the enmity, that is the law of commandments contained in ordinances, so as to create in Himself one new man from the two, thus making peace....by therefore putting to death the enmity".

Wow! Paul is laying out the truth of the Jerusalem Council and the Councils decisions regarding Gentiles and the New Covenant. Please remember what Paul proclaimed at Corinth regarding the Old Covenant. He now enters the next city, Ephesus, and lays the same foundation for Gentile believers in Christ to follow. Please remember the decision to abstain from the shedding of blood. As I have mentioned before could this possibly be referring to circumcision also? I say it was. Circumcision was a cutting away of the flesh, shedding of blood was a part of the Old Covenant. He stated that we the Gentiles are called the uncircumcision, by the so-called circumcision (Jews). The Jews are known as the so called circumcision, the Gentiles were known as the uncircumcision. Paul says that the circumcision was made by human hands. The Gentiles are now circumcised in the heart by the Holy Spirit of the Living God. No longer by the shedding of blood of human or animal flesh, but only by the blood of Christ once for all! We Gentiles were foreigners and aliens to the promises and Covenant of God, but now in the New Covenant through the blood of Christ we have been brought near to God. Jesus has taken the enmity out of the way. The law contained in ordinances and the Old Covenant has been removed. Many say Jesus did not come to abolish the law but he came to fulfill it. This is another partial truth and misunderstanding of the Covenants. After Jesus fulfilled the law he took it out of the way having nailed it to the cross. **Ephesians 2:14:** " For He Himself is our peace, who has made both groups into one, and has broken down the middle wall of separation, **having abolished in His flesh the enmity,** that is the Law of commandments contained in ordinances, so as to create in Himself one new man....."He took the Old Covenant out of the way with its laws, commandments and ordinances and nailed it to the cross in His flesh. Jesus had to first fulfill the law; in order to be able to remove it. **Ephesians**

2:19: "Therefore you are no longer strangers and foreigners, but fellow citizens and members of the household of God, having been built on the foundation of the apostles and prophets, Christ Jesus himself being the chief cornerstone, in whom the whole building, being fitted together, grows into a Holy Temple in the Lord." These Gentiles were being built on the foundation of the apostles and prophets. What was that foundation? We know it was Christ, but what was the Gospel of Christ? It was the Jerusalem Council and the decrees that were decided on by the Holy Spirit. That was the foundational truth that they were delivering to all of the New Covenant Gentile believers. The Old Covenant was built on Mosaic/ Levitical law, and Circumcision. People will not argue or dispute that. They will defend Moses and the Old Covenant laws. If you mention the New Covenant, the Jerusalem Council, and the four decrees people do not YET know how to deal with that truth?

Let's look closer at Ephesians 3 to establish this truth. **Ephesians 3:1-6:** "For this reason I, Paul, the prisoner of Jesus Christ **for you Gentiles**- if indeed you have heard of the dispensation of grace that was given to me for you, how that by revelation He made known to me the mystery (as I have already written in brief by which when you read you can understand my insight into the mystery of Christ), which in other generations was not made known to the sons as it has now been revealed by the Holy Spirit to the Holy apostles and prophets: to be specific the Gentiles are heirs, of the same body, partakers of the promises in Christ through the gospel..."

Can you see it more clearly now in these scriptures? Paul was a prisoner of Jesus Christ for the Gentiles, a specified New Covenant body of believers. This was in accordance to the dispensation of Grace. By revelation God made known this mystery to Paul. What was the mystery? That there was a New Covenant and the Gentiles could be saved and filled with the Holy Spirit. When did he write to them in brief regarding the Gentiles and their position in the New Covenant? The answer is Acts 19, when he delivered the letter to those at Ephesus regarding the decisions that the Holy Spirit made at the Jerusalem Council. Who made the decisions and decrees regarding the Gentile believers in Acts 15? As just stated in **Ephesians 3:5**: "As it has now been revealed by the **Holy Spirit**." The Holy Spirit was there that day during the Jerusalem Council. Acts15:28: "For it seemed good to the **Holy Spirit** and to us, to lay upon you no greater burden than these necessary things." The Holy Spirit made the decisions regarding the four decrees, the New Covenant four commandments of God for Gentiles to abstain from following.

Paul then writes as in all the other epistles how we are to walk worthy of our calling. Do not use this revelation of the Jerusalem Council as a license to sin. **Ephesians 4:17**: "This I say therefore, do not walk as the rest of the other Gentiles walk, in the futility of their mind, having their understanding darkened being alienated from the life of God, because of the ignorance that is in them, because of the blindness of their heart..." Once we understand the Jerusalem Council and our position in Christ, we will not walk and behave like other Gentiles. If a person is truly born again you will see the difference in their life and how they conduct themselves. People should see a difference in us after we accept Jesus Christ. **Ephesians 5:1**: "Therefore, be imitators of God as dear children". How were they to do that, and how are we to do it? Would Paul go on to mention anything from the Jerusalem Council? **Ephesians 5:3**: "But fornication and all uncleanness let it not even be named among you, as is fitting for the saints....." **Ephesians 5:5**, "For this you know, no **fornicator**, unclean person, **covetous man who is an idolater** has any inheritance in the Kingdom of God". The Jerusalem Council made decisions and decrees regarding circumcision, the law, fornication (sexual immorality), idolatry, things strangled and blood.

** Lets list important issues that Paul addresses to the church at Ephesus that were established at the Jerusalem Council.

- He was an apostle to the Gentiles
- Circumcision (Gentiles called uncircumcised?)

Ephesians Receive The Jerusalem Councils Decisions (acts 19)

- Uncircumcision are the Gentiles
- Who are Gentiles under New Covenant
- Law, The Old Covenant law was the enmity
- Law was abolished at the cross
- The Holy Spirit revealed the position of the Gentiles in the New Covenant at the Jerusalem Council
- Fornication (Jerusalem Council)
- Idolatry (Jerusalem Council)

Finally, in the next chapter we are going to look at the last journey Paul made to Jerusalem, and what changes were made to the first Jerusalem Council? How did the Jews feel about what Paul was preaching? How did Paul view the decisions of the Jerusalem Council now? Were the Gentiles to circumcise their children according to the customs of Moses? Were the Gentiles to observe the laws of Moses? Were the Gentiles to observe the decrees that were established by the Holy Spirit at the first Jerusalem Council? Did they add to or take away from the decrees that the Holy Spirit decided on at the first Jerusalem Council? Did the apostles, prophets, and Paul himself still go to the temple and make blood sacrifices after the Jewish believers made the decrees for the Gentiles to follow? All of these questions will be answered in Paul's final journey to Jerusalem, the second Jerusalem council.

13.

Paul's final Journey and the Second Jerusalem Council

I know that I previously stated that **Acts 15** the First Jerusalem Council was my favorite chapter concerning the first Jerusalem Council. If I had to choose any other chapter as my favorite chapter in the New Covenant I would choose **Acts 21** describing the second Jerusalem Council and Paul's final journey. Now you might be thinking why **Acts 21**? It is not one of the most popular chapters in the New Covenant yet I personally believe that some day it will be.

It is the second Jerusalem Council meeting regarding the four decrees and the Gentiles position in the New Covenant. **If anything had changed regarding the first Jerusalem Council and the four decrees we would be able to see it at this final meeting. Acts 20:16,** "...for Paul was hurrying to be at Jerusalem, if possible on the day of Pentecost". Interesting how this entire revelation started at the Feast of Pentecost and the establishment of the first New Covenant Church. Here we are at the end of Paul's life and he still desires to be in Jerusalem on the Feast of Pentecost. **This tells us that Paul (as a Messianic Jew) was still celebrating the Feasts of the Lord.** This is why the Feasts were mentioned in the beginning. **2 Timothy 2:15 (KJV),**" **study to shew thyself approved unto God, a workman that needeth not to be ashamed, rightly dividing the word of truth."** It is extremely important to learn and understand that the Jews, Messianic Jews, Gentiles, and Christians view the exact same scriptures, but honor them differently. Remember how I showed the three views concerning the Feasts of the Lord in the early chapters of this book? How the Jews, and Messianic Jews view the exact same feasts in a different manner than the Gentiles. Jews and Messianic Jews still migrate back to the Old Covenant, circumcision, the Torah, Tanakh, and the Law of Moses. Paul was not preaching against all of these foundational truths regarding the Jews position in the Old Covenant. We will see through **Acts 21** that Paul never preached how the Messianic Jews had to or should view the Old Covenant any differently regarding Circumcision and the observance of the Mosaic Law. **The Jews needed to view the Covenants differently because they definitely need to accept Jesus Christ as their Lord and Savior!** What Paul taught according to the Jerusalem Council to the Gentile believers was different than what he told and taught the Jews. **Acts 21:4**: "they told Paul through the spirit not to go up to Jerusalem". **Acts 21:12**: "Now when we heard these things, both we and those from that place pleaded with him not to go back up to Jerusalem." **Acts 21:13** says Paul was ready to die at Jerusalem. **Acts 21:17**: "When we had come up to Jerusalem the brethren received us gladly. On the following day Paul went in with us to James, and all the elders were present. He proceeded to tell them all that God had done among **the Gentiles** through his ministry". Notice how Paul always determines and clarifies if he is speaking of "things" concerning Jews, Messianic Jew, or Gentiles. **Acts 21:20**, "You see brother how many myriads of **Jews** there are here, and they are zealous for the law." **This is exactly the same as it was in the beginning at the Jerusalem Council.** There were myriads of Jews in Jerusalem on the day of Pentecost. Why? Because this was one of the traveling feasts that Old Covenant required all men and leaders of the house to go to Jerusalem. So all of the Jews and Messianic Jews were in Jerusalem for this feast, they were all zealous for the law.

Acts 21:21, "They have been informed about you that you teach all the Jews (Jew and Messianic Jew) who are among the Gentiles to forsake Moses. Saying that they (Jews and Messianic Jews) ought not to circumcise their children or walk according to the laws of Moses."

Where have we heard this before? **Acts 15:5** tells us that there were some of the sect of the Pharisees who had believed (Messianic Jews), they were saying the Gentiles had to circumcise their children and the Gentiles were to observe the laws of Moses in order to be saved?

Remember these two questions that had to be answered at the first Jerusalem Council?

1. **Were Gentile believers supposed to circumcise their children?**
2. **Were Gentiles to observe the Law of Moses?**

These same issues were the reason why the first Jerusalem Council had to meet. **So what changed if anything regarding the decisions of the first Jerusalem Council meeting, and this meeting at the end of Paul's journeys? Nothing changed concerning the Gentiles position.**

Acts 21:23, "Do what we tell you: we have for men who have taken a vow (this was an Old Testament Nazerite vow that Jews would take). Take them and be purified with them, and pay their expenses so that they may shave their heads and all may know that the things of which they were told concerning you are nothing but that you also walk orderly and keep the law." **ACTS 21:25, "But concerning Gentiles who have believed, we have written that they should observe no such thing**, except that they should keep themselves free from things contaminated by idols, from blood, from things strangled, and from sexual immorality." Can you see the difference between Jews, Messianic Jews, Gentiles and Christians? Paul clearly shows the distinguishing difference here at the end of his journeys. The Holy Spirit determined these four decrees at the first Jerusalem Council. According to these scriptures **nothing had changed** from the first Jerusalem Council to Paul's last journey and the second Jerusalem Council.

Timeline:
- A.D. 31 *Jesus spends 40 days with disciples teaching them things concerning the Kingdom after His resurrection (Acts 1:3-6).
- 10 days later at the Feast of Pentecost the first New Testament Messianic Jewish church was established in Jerusalem (Acts 2)
- A.D. 43 * Gentile Pentecost/ 12 ½ years later after the Day of Pentecost, Peter has the Great Sheet revelation and preaches at Cornelius house. First time Gentiles are filled with the Holy Spirit and speak in tongues (Acts 10: 1-45)
- A.D. 43-46 Paul and Barnabus preach in Antioch for three years and Disciples are called Christians for the first time (Acts 14:16-28).
- A.D. 55-56 / 12 ½ years after Gentile Pentecost and 25 years after the Messianic Jewish Pentecost the First Jerusalem Council takes place!
- (Acts 15:16-31) Paul separates from Barnabus chooses Timothy
- For 3 years Paul and Timothy journey through the cities delivering the decrees of the Jerusalem Council
- A.D. 58-60 Second Jerusalem Council (Acts 21:18-26). Nothing changes regarding the Decrees the Holy Spirit decided on for Gentile believers.

The decision and decrees that were decided on by the Holy Spirit were never changed. Paul proclaimed them at the first Jerusalem Council as well as the second Jerusalem Council. It is clear to see at the end of Paul's journeys they were still standing firm on the first Jerusalem Council's decisions and the decrees that were made regarding the Gentile believers in Christ. Please understand the first Jerusalem Council and the decrees that were decided on were not directed at the Jews or Messianic Jewish people -but specifically regarding the Gentiles and what the Gentiles were to do. This is why Paul, being a Messianic Jew, still walked orderly and kept the law. **But concerning the Gentiles (Acts 21:25)**, they immediately refer back to the first Jerusalem Council meeting and the four decrees that the Holy Spirit had decided. The non-believing Jews hated Paul because they thought he was teaching things contrary to the Jews Old Covenant and the Laws of Moses. He was not. Paul understood completely the decisions that were made regarding the Gentile believers in Christ at the first Jerusalem Council. He was there at the first Jerusalem Council. In Acts 15:28 Paul knew the Holy Spirit made these decisions regarding the Gentile believers in Christ. These decisions were not made regarding Jews. **As mentioned earlier every one of these groups could see the same glass half full, or half empty. They see the same glass, same amount of water, but come to different conclusions. What I mean by this is they can see the same scriptures, but interpret them differently, and come to different conclusion.** This is why it is so important to know how to rightly divide the Word of Truth! Paul understood that there are two different Covenants that are viewed differently by four different groups of people.

As we grow closer to the coming of the Messiah more Jews will be converted to Messianic Jews and it will be extremely important for all groups to know how to rightly divide the Word of Truth. Messianic Jews in their excitement will try to pull Gentiles back into following the Laws of the Old Covenant. Gentiles will never be able to fulfill the Old Covenant. The exact same two questions might arise again regarding circumcision and the Law of Moses. This is why as we increase in knowledge it is so vitally important to know how to rightly divide the Word of Truth.

14.

Conclusion of the Jerusalem Council.

*I*n summary, we see that Jesus had to come back for forty days and teach the disciples "things" concerning the kingdom of God. He spent 40 days teaching the disciples in His resurrected, supernatural body. The Feast of Pentecost was fulfilled 10 days after this 40 day period, for a total of 50 days (or Pente meaning fifty). The first Messianic Jewish New Covenant church was established at Jerusalem **at the Feast of Pentecost**. This church primarily consisted of Messianic Jews and some Gentile proselytes. It was not until twelve and a half years later that Peter received the Great Sheet Revelation. Peter was divinely sent by an angel to Cornelius's house (please read Acts 10). For the first time in history a group of Gentiles was converted and received the Holy Spirit with the evidence of speaking in tongues. This was approximately twelve and a half years after the day of Pentecost. The Messianic Jews were amazed because this was the first time in History that such an event had ever happened. **(NKJV) Acts 10:44-46, "While Peter was speaking these words, the Holy Spirit fell upon all those who heard the word, and those of the circumcision (Messianic Jews) who had believed were astonished, as many as came with Peter, because the gift of the Holy Spirit had been poured out on the Gentiles also. For they heard them speak with tongues and magnify God"**. The Gentile believers received the Holy Spirit with the evidence of speaking in tongues;

therefore the disciples were first called Christians at Antioch. I call this the second New Covenant Church; this church primarily consisted of Gentile Christians. Now we have Messianic Jews in the first New Covenant church at Jerusalem, and Gentile Christians in the second New Covenant Church at Antioch. The Messianic Jews eventually ran into a problem regarding the position of the Gentiles. These issues or problems were dealt with at the Jerusalem Council. Twelve years after the first Gentile church was established at Antioch, the first Jerusalem Council meeting was held. **The Jerusalem Council meeting was also 25 years after Pentecost and the establishing of the first Messianic Jewish New Covenant Church.** After a twenty-five year period the Jews who had believed were still teaching the Gentile believers they had to be circumcised and they had to observe the laws of Moses in order to be saved. These two headquarters consisted of Messianic Jews at Jerusalem and Gentile Christians at the church at Antioch. This meeting was called the Jerusalem Council. **At this council the Holy Spirit decided on four specific commandments, or decrees from which the Gentiles were to abstain from.**

<u>Please remember Decree | Definition of Decree by Merriam-Webster</u>

> Legal Definition. 1: an order having the force of law by judicial decree. 2: a judicial decision especially in an equity or probate court broadly: judgment divorce decree interlocutory decree.

- **By definition, "A decree is an official order issued by a legal authority. Synonyms are listed here: order, edict a command, or a commandment, a proclamation."**

These commandments were put in the form of a letter. Paul the apostle to the Gentiles took this letter with Timothy and delivered it to the Gentile Christian churches. **Paul and Timothy delivered**

Conclusion Of The Jerusalem Council.

the Jerusalem Councils letter to the following cities: Galatia, Philippi, Thessalonica, Corinth, Ephesus, Rome, and finally back to Jerusalem. At the end of all his life-risking journeys, Paul had to go to Jerusalem again on the Feast of Pentecost.

I call this the second Jerusalem Council. There the Jews thought he taught "things" contrary to the Old Covenant, such as circumcision and the laws of Moses. Therefore, the apostles and elders from the first Messianic Jewish New Covenant Church at Jerusalem advised Paul to go to the temple and make a blood sacrifice and to a make a vow with four men. Paul listened to their advice. Was he transgressing the Jerusalem Councils decisions regarding abstaining from blood, Circumcision, and the laws of Moses? Absolutely not. It was perfectly fine and legal for a Messianic Jew to still enter into the temple and make a blood sacrifice as well as make a pledge. The Jew and Messianic Jews were still going into the temple and making sacrifices for approximately 40 years until the temple was destroyed in 70A.D. If it were not legal and right Paul, a Messianic Jew would not have entered the temple and made a blood sacrifice. **Remember this is at the end of Paul's journeys; nothing had changed regarding the decisions and decrees the Holy Spirit made at the first Jerusalem Council.** The position of Jews, Messianic Jews, Gentiles, and Gentile Christians were different. The Messianic Jew, in this case Paul, could go to the Temple and make a blood sacrifice. Could a Gentile have done this? Absolutely not! This is exactly what the Jerusalem Council decided. Gentiles were to abstain from the shedding of blood; therefore, Gentiles could not offer any blood sacrifices according to the decrees that the Holy Spirit decided on for the Gentile believers in the New Covenant.

Here is a thought to consider that might happen before the coming of the Lord. Remember one difference between then and now is there is no Temple in Jerusalem. I believe when there is a Temple the Jews and many Messianic Jews will immediately begin animal sacrifices as Paul and the other disciples did in the beginning. This is just one example that can be used to show the difference in position for the Jews, Messianic Jews, Gentiles, and Gentile Christians under the same covenant.

Remember in the early church the majority, Messianic Jews ushered in the Gentiles and in the last days the majority, Gentiles will usher in the Messianic Jews. As we approach the end of the age the third temple will be built, and the Jews will begin to offer sacrifices again. In my opinion the Messianic Jews will also partake in these sacrifices, just as Paul did in Jerusalem at the end of his journeys. This was approximately in 58-60 A.D. and Paul was still making sacrifices in the temple. The second temple was destroyed in 70A.D. Therefore, in order to offer sacrifices again the third temple must be rebuilt. **Revelation 11:2 (KJV):** "But the court which is outside the temple leave out and measure it not; for it is given unto the Gentiles and the Holy City shall they tread under foot for forty-two months." **In order to measure the temple, the third temple must be rebuilt.** After the abomination of desolation sets himself up in the temple, there will be 42 months left. **Revelation 13:5 New King James Version (NKJV)** [5] And he was given a mouth speaking great things and blasphemies, and he was given authority to continue for forty-two months. Forty –two months is exactly three and a half years. The process of restoration will be completed according to **Acts 3:21** (NAS 1977): "Whom heaven must receive until the period of restoration of all things…"

At the Jerusalem Council the Holy Spirit decided on four decrees, or commandments from which the Gentiles to abstain from. In these last days, Jews, Messianic Jews, Gentiles, and Gentile Christians will come to the full understanding of the Jerusalem Council. This understanding will help Gentile Christians better understand the position of Messianic Jews. Messianic Jews will better understand the position of the Gentiles in the New Covenant. This is exactly what happened in the early church, and it is getting ready to happen again. This will bring the period of restoration to an end and the Messiah will return to set up His Kingdom on this earth for 1,000 years.

Conclusion Of The Jerusalem Council.

Maranatha, come quickly Lord Jesus!

All scripture and quotes are taken from the New King James Bible unless specifically stated otherwise.

www.ingramcontent.com/pod-product-compliance
Ingram Content Group UK Ltd.
Pitfield, Milton Keynes, MK11 3LW, UK
UKHW022221230426
12048UKWH00016BA/982